Insight Text Guide

by

Scott Hurley

BA, MA, PhD

NO GREAT MISCHIEF

Alistair MacLeod

First published in 2001, reprinted 2004.

Insight Publications Pty Ltd
ACN 005 102 983
ABN 57 005 102 983
Suite 1, 128 Balcombe Road,
Mentone Vic 3194
Australia.
Tel.: 03 9583 5839
Fax: 03 9583 9573

email: books@insightpublications.com.au

www.vceenglish.com

Cover Design: Richard Chambers
DTP: Geoffrey Heard & Associates (03) 9583 0788
Editing: Elli Lewis
Printing: Shannon Books Victoria.

Hurley, Scott

Insight text guide: No Great Mischief

ISBN 1 875882 73 1

CONTENTS

MAIN CHARACTERS

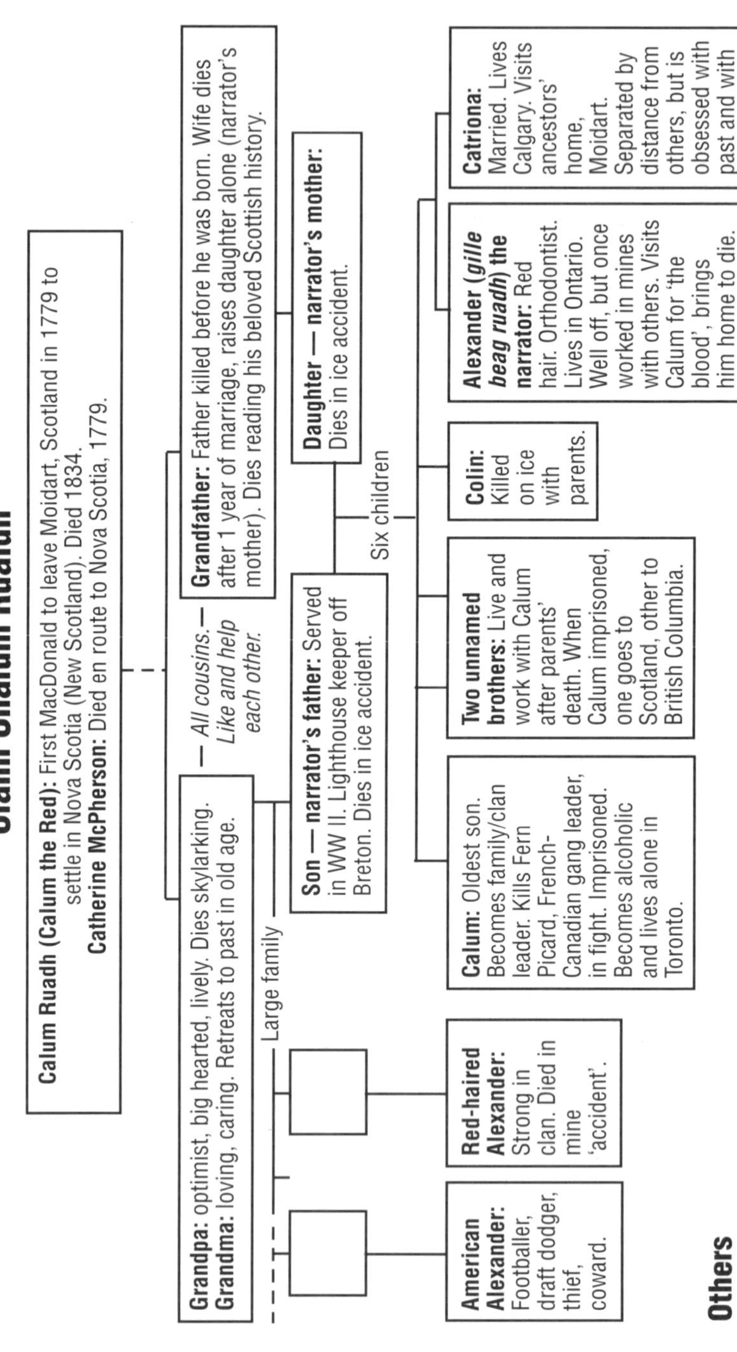

INTRODUCTION

Born in Saskatchewan, Canada, in 1936, Alistair MacLeod moved with his family to Cape Breton, Nova Scotia, at the age of ten. Working during summers either logging or mining to pay for his education, MacLeod earned a PhD in English from the University of Notre Dame in 1968. He recently retired from his position as Professor of English and Creative Writing at the University of Windsor in Ontario. Though admired in Canada for two volumes of short stories, MacLeod was little known to the rest of the world until his first novel, *No Great Mischief*, was published to great acclaim in 1999. It won the Trillum Prize and the IMPAC Dublin Literary Award in 2001.

No Great Mischief is the story of the *clann Chalum Ruaidh*, a fictional branch of the great Scottish clan of MacDonald, in Cape Breton, Nova Scotia. The novel follows three generations, each marked somehow by tragedy. Before the narrator's[1] Grandfather was born, his father was killed while logging in the woods of Maine, and in later life he buries his wife and daughter at very young ages. In the next generation, the narrator's parents are killed in a tragic accident; he and his four surviving siblings must struggle to create lives for themselves after so great a loss. This proves hardest for the eldest son, Calum, who continues the 'tragedy' in the third generation when he kills a man in a fight outside a uranium mine in Ontario.

Even before this event, Calum is associated with some of the more tragic leaders of the MacDonald clan, his ancient forebears. Though introverted by nature, Calum must wear the mantle of leadership that descends upon him after the death of his parents. *No Great Mischief* is the story of how the constraints of leadership can impact negatively on a life; we see this all the more clearly through the eyes of Calum's youngest brother, the narrator, whose life could be said to be 'lucky' in comparison. However, each member of the clan, in each generation, is somehow haunted by the past. Some revisit the glorious victories and defeats of the ancient Highlanders and thus make them a part of their very different lives; some look to the past as shelter *against* modern life. We readers come to see the ways in which the past repeats itself, and how it can be a burden to those trying to live in the modern world.

1 The narrator's name is Alexander MacDonald, but he is rarely called that. Because there are other characters named Alexander MacDonald, I will refer to the one who tells the story as 'the narrator'.

BACKGROUND & CONTEXT

In order to appreciate the way the characters in *No Great Mischief* understand the past, one must have some knowledge of the Scottish Highlanders.

A Brief Introduction to Clan Donald and Scottish Highlanders

The MacDonalds are the most numerous of the great Scottish Highland clans, many of whom can trace their history back well over a thousand years. (Note: in Gaelic, one of the languages of Scotland before English came to be the dominant language, 'Mac' means 'son of'; thus MacDonald means 'son of Donald'.) The Highlands, in the northern part of the country, is very rugged, mountainous terrain marked by lakes and moors. It is not particularly suitable to farming or animal husbandry. This is one of many reasons why the 'old ways' of the clans, those of a warrior society, survived well into the 17th century. Scotland's history is a very bloody one, and the Highlands have seen some of the worst fighting, against Britons, Danes and Norwegian raiders, and most commonly, amongst the clans themselves. The great clans became powerful by training their men to be excellent fighters, and by engaging regularly in battle.

The Highlanders played their part in most of the frequent political upheavals in Scotland's history. There has always been a rivalry between them and the people of the Scottish Lowlands; the Lowlands were populated by clans as well, but for a number of reasons (the land is much better for farming, for example), the Lowlands were much more adaptable to modern living. Most of the stereotypical images often associated with Scottish tradition — the castles in the mist, the lone piper in tartan, the epic battles between fierce warriors — are really stereotypes of the Highlands.

It would be impossible to cover all of the history of the Highlands, but we should mention some of the events that the characters in *No Great Mischief* mention specifically. Most of them took place within a hundred year span, from the late 1600s to the late 1700s, a period of great upheaval for a nation about to finally lose the battle against its ancient foe. Scotland had been at war on and off with England since about the 12th century; by the end of the 17th century, England was coming into its full dominance over the Scots, but there was still resistance, particularly from the Highlanders. Much of the political climate of the time had to do with the contested succession to the English throne. The Highlanders were firmly behind the cause of Jacobism: the restoration of the Catholic Stuarts (in exile in France) to the Crown of both countries (most of the Stuart, or Stewart, kings were named James—hence the Latin 'Jacobite'). Needless to say, this pitted the Highlanders against the Hanoverian English monarchs. They met in battle a number of times. One occasion (mentioned in *Chapter 13*) was at the pass of Killiecrankie, where in July of 1689 the Highlanders, under their leader 'Bonnie Dundee', ambushed and killed forces of King William. 'Dundee' was killed, however, and not long after, the Highlanders were routed at Dunkeld.

The Massacre of Glencoe

Another incident, mentioned several times in the novel, was the massacre at Glencoe in 1692. As the narrator tells it, this branch of the MacDonald clan were set upon by troops whom they had quartered for two weeks under orders from the 'Master of Stair' (the Secretary of State). It had been proclaimed that those clans who had taken arms against King William three years earlier would be pardoned if they took an oath of allegiance to the Crown before 1 January 1692. Mac Ian, the head of the MacDonalds of Glencoe, was deemed a few days late in making his oath (he had apparently tried to take this oath on time); it was decided that his clan would be made an example. Thirty-eight MacDonalds were murdered on the morning of 13 February 1692.

Bonnie Prince Charlie

In 1707, Scotland was officially joined with England and Wales. Though it maintained a good deal of autonomy, it would not govern itself again. Two more Jacobite uprisings occurred in 1715 and in 1745. They are known as *the '15* and *the '45*. The latter was the more serious and consequential of the two; its failure signalled the end of the Jacobite claim on the English and Scottish thrones. *The '45* is mentioned a number of times in *No Great Mischief*. It is implied that clan patriarch *Calum Ruadh*, who was 21 at the time, took up the call to 'follow Charlie'. This refers to Prince Charles Edward Stuart, or 'Bonnie Prince Charlie', who landed in England from France that year (while much of the British Army was otherwise occupied with the War of the Austrian Succession) hoping to gain the English throne.

Prince Charlie managed to draw a number of recruits in the Highlands — including the MacDonalds — and made war on the British. Victory at the

Battle of Prestonpans encouraged him to march on London with a force of 5,000, but could make it no farther than Derby. Prince Charlie never managed to attract many followers outside the Highlands (many from the Lowlands did not join for this very reason). The rebellion never really had a chance without the help of the French, who had been allies with the Scots in the past against the English (referred to as *the auld alliance*). No French ships landed with reinforcements for the cause. A year later, Charlie's forces were routed by the English under the Duke of Cumberland at Culloden in Northern Scotland, a battle mentioned several times in the novel.

Why Highlanders Emigrated

After Culloden, things became far more precarious for the Highlanders. This is the period when *Calum Ruadh* emigrates with his family to Canada, as did many from the Highland clans. Their traditional way of life was becoming untenable. There was very little to do for so many men raised on war but emigrate and start over in the New World. Those who did not, threw in their lot with their enemy, Britain, as soldiers for the empire. Ironically, the enemy they faced was their old ally, France. Little more than ten years after *the '45*, the British were embroiled with France in a far-reaching conflict known as the Seven Years' War. Its North America theatre, fought mostly in Canada, was known as the French and Indian War because the French were allied with a number of great North American Indian tribes.

General James Wolfe and 'No great mischief'

One of the key players in the French and Indian War was General James Wolfe, referred to many times in the novel as a model of treachery. Wolfe was sent to capture the city of Quebec held by the forces of the Marquis de Montcalm. After laying siege for about two months, Wolfe tried a cunning tactic, ordering his forces to scale the cliffs surrounding the city; forcing Montcalm out of the city. The Battle of the Plains of Abraham soon followed on 13 September 1759; it lasted less than an hour and was a victory for the British, winning them Quebec. In the battle both Montcalm and Wolfe were killed. A year later the British had won all of Canada.

In their discussions of the Plains of Abraham, characters in the novel focus on the role of the Highlanders in scaling the cliffs of Quebec and winning victory. They also deliberate over this irony: as a young man of 19, Wolfe had perhaps fought against these same Highlanders at Culloden. His treachery — at least in the eyes of the novel's characters — comes from a private remark he had made about the Highlanders after he took command of them, that it was 'no great mischief' if they fell. In other words, he did not really trust the Highlanders, experienced as they were at fighting. To Wolfe they were expendable.

It is a question for historians whether Wolfe gets fair treatment in this novel. He was certainly a heroic figure. Only 32 and mortally ill with tuberculosis when he undertook the campaign in Quebec, he won a stunning victory over the more seasoned Montcalm. And though much is made of the loyalty of the Highlanders in *No Great Mischief*, Wolfe would surely have had some reason to be wary of men under his command whom he had faced as enemies only 14 years before. Without question, rightly or wrongly, he would have seen the Highlanders as little more than mercenaries (even if they were now British citizens); a view commonly held by most commanders of that age towards 'hired troops'.

Nova Scotia

Many of the migrating Scots settled in Nova Scotia (in Latin it means 'New Scotland'), one of the maritime provinces of Canada and home to a thriving shipping industry based in the capital, Halifax. The family in the novel, the *clann Chalum Ruaidh*, settles in Cape Breton, a large island off the north coast of Nova Scotia. There were times in history when Cape Breton had its own dominion, but in 1820 it was permanently united with Nova Scotia. Nova Scotia has topographical similarities to Scotland, though it is more forested. Ninety percent of the land is unsuitable for agriculture. Work would have revolved either around the sea or logging or mining. Cape Breton is known for its own 'Highlands', mountainous and forested, as well as its rocky coastline. It would have been a difficult place to scratch out a living for the new migrants, but one imagines that there was much reason for them to feel 'at home'. And this no doubt explains some of the persistence of traditional Scottish culture in Cape Breton even today, including the study of Gaelic.

Nova Scotia was not untouched by the French and Indian War; a battle was fought on Cape Breton. Not mentioned in *No Great Mischief*, but of historical importance, is a small but disturbing chapter in the history of the British Empire. The first European settlers to arrive in Nova Scotia in 1605 were French; they called the area Acadia after the local Micmac Indian name for it. After a long dispute between France and England over the territory, it was awarded to Britain in 1713 under the Treaty of Utrecht (this is when it was renamed Nova Scotia).

In 1750, the descendants of the original French settlers were expelled from Nova Scotia when they refused to swear loyalty to the British and adopt Protestantism. This expulsion was particularly brutal; families were intentionally split up and put on different ships without any idea of their destination. Needless to say, many never saw each other again. A large number of these exiles found their way eventually to Louisiana — at that time a French colony — where they stuck together and became known as 'Cajuns' (the local pronunciation of 'Acadians'). They live there to this day. Though not mentioned at all in the novel, this episode has many parallels to the central events of *No Great Mischief*.

GENRE, STYLE & STRUCTURE

Genre

No Great Mischief maintains a consistent narrative voice; only one person tells the story — the narrator, Alexander MacDonald. He uses *recalled* dialogue quite frequently for the purpose of letting characters speak with their own voice. As readers we make a kind of 'contract' with authors; here we must agree to accept that the narrator's memory is so powerful as to be able to remember what people said years earlier. But few other demands are made on our credulity in *No Great Mischief*. This is a realist novel. It is not beyond our belief that all the events in the novel could have actually happened.

A Realist Novel

As a realist novel, *No Great Mischief* puts itself in a certain position of authority. When authors tell a very realistic story, they are usually trying to convey a particular viewpoint. We are expected to accept this viewpoint as believable, accurate, and thus applicable to our own lives. *Naturalism*, a school of writing which first came into prominence in the late 19th century, espoused very realistic writing as a refreshing technique at a time of conventionality, and as an instrument of social change. *No Great Mischief* is not a work of *Naturalism* in this sense (its writing aspires too much to a poetic quality for that), nor does it seem to want to reform society. Yet its believability does demand a certain attention. It tells us that this is a 'real' story about the desires, the failings, the joys, the sorrows etc., of 'real' people. Indirectly it tells us also that their story has bearing on our own lives. Another intention is that because the story is so believable, the opinions presented in it must be valid. This does not mean that MacLeod's book contains propaganda, but this is one of the characteristics of realism — its believability automatically lends its message a kind of authority that non-realistic writing cannot so easily achieve.

Style

No Great Mischief is a serious novel which indicates that it has an important point to convey (see THEMES & ISSUES for further discussion). It is not humourless, but having a fairly tragic message about loss of cultural heritage and the repetition of the past, its language tends to be serious and dignified. MacLeod also tries for an elevated or poetic tone. Sometimes it is successful (see the last chapter), other times it is less so (for instance in the metaphorical comparisons in the first paragraph of p.67). The writing seems to work best when MacLeod sticks to a realistic, detailed description, as in, for example, the account of the uranium mine in *Chapter 21*.

MacLeod often uses metaphorical constructions for symbolic purposes. This happens most frequently when the narrator's brother Calum is indirectly compared to some natural element like the spring of fresh water on the island where his father was the lighthouse keeper, or the pilot whale who swam too close to shore (see CHAPTER-BY-CHAPTER ANALYSIS for more examples). Again, these comparisons are not explicit (the narrator never writes 'my brother Calum was just like the pilot whale'); it is up to the reader to interpret these connections. The novel is full of such symbols. We are often encouraged to associate the characters with objects or animals written about in an otherwise straightforward, realistic way. *No Great Mischief* is a good example of how symbolism can be used in realistic fiction.

Structure

No Great Mischief is composed of three narrative strands occurring over different times. Its chapters alternate, in no predictable sequence, among:

- the episode in which the narrator visits Calum in Toronto and goes to buy him some beer;
- the conversation he had two years earlier with his sister in her house in Calgary; and
- the general history of the narrator and his family.

The final strand is of course the most extensive. It includes the history of the clan in Nova Scotia, the history of his grandparents' generation, his parents' lives and deaths and the story of the fateful summer of 1968 at the uranium mine. This is interrupted fairly often by the two other strands, making the narrative seem rather strained at times; the narrator seems to be forever out buying a case of beer for Calum. Those chapters in modern-day Toronto and Calgary serve the purpose of continually juxtaposing the present with the past, but there is a feeling at times that that is the *only* reason they are there, as interruptions to the main and more interesting story.

CHAPTER-BY-CHAPTER ANALYSIS

Chapter 1 (pp.1-15)

Summary: *Alexander MacDonald visits his oldest brother Calum in a rooming house in modern-day Toronto.*

The novel opens in Canada with the narrator driving from his home in the province of Ontario to the capital city Toronto, a drive he makes weekly to see his oldest brother, Calum. Calum is an advanced alcoholic, living a rootless existence apparently driven by alcohol and memories.

It is autumn, harvest time. The narrator sees migrant workers harvesting, picking fruit; the workers and what they are doing are important symbols to him. We learn he is middle-aged, in life's autumn, telling us his story, 'harvesting' his memories. Calum is in 'winter', obviously near death. And like Calum, the *clann Chalum Ruaidh* — the clan of *Calum Ruadh* (Calum the Red) the first MacDonald to settle in Nova Scotia (New Scotland) — is clinging tenuously to life.

This novel is about the past. Many of the characters are so haunted by the past that they can hardly function. The narrator implies as much in the closing of the chapter when he imagines himself being pulled in one direction by the 20th century and in another by the past as embodied by his brother Calum.

Chapter 2 (pp.16-24)

Summary: Calum Ruadh*'s history is described.*

We find out why the narrator is called *gille beag ruadh*. It is Gaelic for 'the little red-haired boy'. The offspring of *clann Chalum Ruaidh* are dark-eyed and have either jet-black or red hair. The narrator hardly knows his 'real' name, Alexander MacDonald, being much more familiar with *gille beag ruadh.* This shows how strongly the descendants of Scottish migrants in Nova Scotia have held on to their heritage, even to the present.

We learn about *Calum Ruadh*, the founder of the clan in Nova Scotia. He left Scotland in 1779, a tumultuous period in the history of Europe (see BACKGROUND & CONTEXT). Events in the 70 year period between 'Bonnie' Prince Charlie in 1745 to Waterloo included the Seven Years' War, the War of American Independence, the French Revolution and the Napoleonic Wars. The Scots, and Highlanders in particular, played their role in each of these conflicts. In each case they were torn between competing loyalties — the choice was never clear. This is evidenced in the brief passage about the Scots in North Carolina fighting on *both* sides in the American Revolution and calling out to one another in the night (p.18). The theme of divided loyalties and difficult choices will be carried over in different form in the narrator's twentieth-century life.

Yet when the choice *is* made, loyalty is total and fiercely pursued. We are meant to see the clan as being just like the dog which swims after *Calum Ruadh's* boat as the clan leave for the ship that will take them to Canada. This dog is an ancestor of the narrator's parents' faithful dog. The narrator remarks how 'that part about the dog' always 'got' to his grandfather (p.20).

This interjection underscores the extent to which the family's history is alive in each member. They are almost obsessed with their shared history; it is this that binds them as a 'clan', an element of the present as well as the past.

This novel is full of symbolism: the narrator remembers hearing the story of his great-great-great-grandfather from his own grandfather as they chopped wood in early spring. He recalls that 'geese were winging northward...seeming fools for being so early yet being geometrically true to their intended course and purpose' (p.21). These geese too, like the dog, are stand-ins for the intrepid *Calum Ruadh* and his descendants.

Chapter 3 (pp.25-28)

Summary: *We learn some more about the importance of* clann Chalum Ruaidh *in Nova Scotia and elsewhere.*

The clan identify themselves and they recognise their own (on account of the dark eyes and red or black hair) as far afield as Calgary, a distance of about 4,000 kilometres. This is the city where the narrator's twin sister, Catriona, has settled.

It is important in understanding the psychology of the narrator and his sister to realise that they have both moved a very long distance away from the ancestral home in Cape Breton, Nova Scotia.

Chapter 4 (pp.29-35)

Summary: *We are introduced to the narrator's three grandparents.*

His father's parents, called 'Grandma' and 'Grandpa', raised the narrator and Catriona from the age of three. Their mother's father is called 'Grandfather'. His wife died giving birth to their mother. Here we see a bit of the 'clan' way; Grandma and Grandpa are cousins — so is Grandfather. What's more, Grandma's sister married Grandpa's brother. This isn't quite incest, but every member of the narrator's immediate family, without exception, is *clann Chalum Ruaidh*.

The two grandfathers, though they are cousins, are a study in contrasts. Grandfather, the older of the two, is neat, precise and meticulous. Grandpa is flamboyant and hearty (see CHARACTER & RELATIONSHIPS). He drinks too much and likes off-colour jokes. Grandfather is upright and sober. Yet when it comes time to do a good turn for the other, Grandfather makes sure that Grandpa is prepared to get a good job as head of maintenance at the new local hospital. As Grandma, who can seem little more than a bundle of old maxims, says of Grandfather, he 'looks after his blood'.

Chapter 5 (pp.36-40)

Summary: *Memories of a Christmas Eve on which Grandma showed how understanding she was about Grandpa's drinking.*

The narrator tells how he often thinks about his grandparents in the same way he thinks about his Scottish ancestry — not as what must be evoked consciously, but something that is always lying under the surface waiting to make itself known. He says this is true even in some of the expensive destinations where he and his family vacation in the winter 'trying to pretend that, for us, there really is no winter' (p.36). We are being asked to contrast the narrator's modern existence (in which he has acquired some wealth as an orthodontist) and his grandparents' simpler but happier life.

Chapter 6 (pp.41-47)

Key Chapter

Summary: *A description of how the narrator's parents died.*

After returning from service in World War II, his father became the lighthouse keeper on an island directly off the coast of Cape Breton. In the cold Canadian winter the water between it and the mainland freezes, allowing passage to the town. On one late March day the entire family (six children and the parents) crossed over with the family dog. That night, the narrator's parents, with one brother, Colin, set off for home (he and his sister were staying over with Grandma and Grandpa, while the three older boys were staying with other relatives). Somewhere on the way they broke through the ice and were drowned. Only the body of Colin is recovered:

> And in the early hours of the morning when the tide was in its change, my brother Colin surfaced in one of those half-expected uncertainties known only to those who watch the sea (p.47).

The lives of the survivors are drastically changed. The narrator and his sister are raised by their grandparents while the three surviving brothers go to live in the old family house.

Chapter 7 (pp.48-53)

Key Chapter

Summary: *All of the clan attend Colin's wake.*

Here we see again an example of 'looking after your blood' (the chapter ends with Grandma saying exactly this). Clan discussions revolve around the 'how' and 'why' of the accident. No satisfactory answer other than 'an act of God' can be discerned for either question (it was a freak break in the ice that sent them to their deaths). Superstitious folk, some of the clan conjecture about what sin the parents must have committed to prompt their early deaths from an angry God. The sad story of the family dog, killed by the 'man from Pictou' is related, recalling the loyalty of the first dog from *Chapter 2* who swam out to join *Calum Ruadh* in the trip across the ocean. This novel is gathering a number of deaths at sea: besides this dog are *Calum Ruadh*'s wife, Catherine MacPherson, who died en route to Canada, and, of course, the narrator's parents. One of the hallmarks of being obsessed with history is seeing how much it repeats itself.

The narrator tells us that this is 'a story of lives which turned out differently than was intended' (p.52). We will see how the lives of the two primary characters, Calum and the narrator, go in very different directions after the deaths of their parents.

Chapter 8 (pp.54-56)

Summary: *In the present. The narrator continues his mission to buy alcohol in Toronto; he remembers an encounter at an orthodontist's convention.*

Looking for alcohol for Calum, the narrator walks through some of Toronto's less celebrated streets. He thinks about the many immigrants in the city as he hears various languages spoken. An anti-nuclear war protest has been occurring that day in Toronto and he recalls some of the signs held by counter-protesters ('If you don't think Canada is worth defending, go somewhere else'). He also remembers an episode at a conference some time earlier where an obnoxious American orthodontist asked the narrator about Ukrainians in Canada and the national health system.

This recollection presents the Texan orthodontist as someone who claims that Ukraine is not marked on the map of Russia and therefore the Ukrainians are in fact Russian. He appears ignorant and blinded by anti-Communism. He is clearly preoccupied with making money, telling Alexander that if he came to Texas he would be able to triple his income because there the rich are 'willing to pay to be beautiful' (p.55). He is a modern man who has accepted his family's name change in order to better fit into the American society — his family heritage is irrelevant to him, unlike the narrator from clan Donald intent on keeping alive his ties with the past.

The Texan also challenges Alexander to declare whether 'you guys consider yourselves Canadians or North Americans first?' (p.55) but does not wait because he anticipates that the answer will be 'it's not that simple'. This issue of the relationship between Canadians and Americans arises again later (see Chapter 33 p.206 in the novel, p.33 in this guide). Here the tone suggests that Canadians need to get straight, and possibly accept, that their country is an extension of America and that they are therefore more rightly North Americans.

While the Texan fulfils many features of the stereotypical Texan, the narrator emerges as someone who is more aware of the complexities of ethnic difference, more tolerant, informed and more devoted to his profession because he is less attached to money.

> ***Q*** You need to consider why this incident is recounted at all. Do you think that this negative picture of the American reveals that Alexander (or the author himself) is guilty of prejudice against Americans, particularly Texans? How do you interpret this interlude?

Another theme in this novel is the fragility of the unchangeable past in the ever-changing present. Thinking about how Calum is destroying himself with alcohol, the narrator recalls something that his grandfather used to say: 'The *clann Chalum Ruaidh* will live for a long time… If they are given the chance and if they want to' (p.56). These words are meaningful both for Calum and for the narrator. By the end of the novel we might be applying the first of the grandfather's conditional statements ('if they are given the chance') to Calum, and the second ('if they want to') to his brother.

The chapter ends with a protester walking by with a slogan on her T-shirt that is even more applicable to the narrator: 'Living in the past is not living up to our potential'. What really haunts this character about the past is the fact that he has turned his back on it to become what he calls a 'twentieth-century man'.

Chapter 9 (pp.57-64)

Summary: *The lives of the surviving children after the deaths of the parents are described.*

Calum and the two other older brothers (they are never given names) go to live in the house that Grandpa and Grandma lived in before they were given 'the chance' (the job at the hospital) and became 'city people'. It is the old homestead of the clan. The narrator and his sister (she is only twice referred to by name) are raised in much more comfortable circumstances in town by these grandparents.

You could say that the narrator and his sister continue in the 20th century while Calum and the others return to the 19th century.

The brothers have to carve their living out of the land and the sea in a house without running water or electricity. They give up school, essentially returning to the life of their ancestors: fishing, cutting wood, hunting, planting. The narrator's later obsession with the past is in part fed by this feeling that his own brothers belong to a completely different culture from his own, even if they are not that far removed by distance. He stays with them for periods in the summer and sometimes in the winter, witnessing their nineteenth-century lives and envying their freedom. He returns to his family's past.

At the end of the chapter the narrator recalls a fight that he once had with one of his many cousins, another Alexander MacDonald, over childish 'ownership' of their shared grandparents. We hear of this cousin later.

Chapter 10 (pp.65-66)

Summary: *Back in the present, the migrant fruit pickers are contrasted with the 'pick-your-own' crowd of Canadian day-trippers and their children.*

It remains to be seen what the full symbolic importance of this contrast is. The first group seems to be symbolically aligned with the 'old way' of the clans, that way of life which the three older brothers must return to; the second group would be associated with the narrator and his sister who fully pursue the comforts of the middle-class in twentieth-century Canada. This distinction is alluded to as the narrator continues to contemplate what alcohol he should buy for Calum and himself, 'for the men who have everything or nothing' (p.66).

Chapter 11 (pp.67-75)

Summary: *The lives of the three brothers are described further.*

The narrator describes the excitement with which he and his sister used to go to visit their brothers in the house by the sea. It was a world full of animals: cows, horses, chickens, sheep, cats and dogs. He relates how his sister began to visit less frequently as they became older. She seems to feel slightly uncomfortable, but not nearly as uncomfortable as they feel around her. There is a suggestion that the brothers are living some kind of 'masculine' life that proves incompatible with 'femininity'. They live a life almost entirely without the formalities of 'polite' society. Their toilet is a bucket, unless they simply urinate out the window. The narrator does not invite us to make judgements, he simply tells us the way it is. The brothers are returning to an existence closer to nature; they have to work hard for what they get, without many of the comforts of civilisation.

The way that this reality affects the personalities of the brothers is exemplified by the incident that ends the chapter. Calum, bothered by an infected tooth, tries to pull it out of his mouth with a pair of pliers. That failing, he straps himself to Christy, the horse, and for even more unorthodox bit of dentistry. We cannot help but see a contrast between Calum and the narrator's later patients who spend a fortune on dentistry for the sake of vanity.

Q Notice how Calum is repeatedly associated with blood (the chapter ends with blood running down his face and into the hair on his chest the way it does in the very first chapter of the novel). What is the symbolic significance?

Chapter 12 (pp.76-78)

Summary: *Some reflections on the narrator's orthodontic practice; a symbolic pigeon.*

As if to reinforce the contrast we noted in the above chapter, the narrator elaborates on his profession as an orthodontist. He implies that the great majority of the work he does is superfluous. Beyond the impacted wisdom teeth and other potentially painful or disfiguring problems, he is mainly trying to appease the vanity of his 'customers'.

Still looking for a bottle of alcohol for his brother, he sees a pigeon missing a foot. It is only noticeably handicapped when it tries to walk; when it flies, it does so unencumbered. But notice how it does not fly away; it returns.

Q Should we be asking ourselves what are the things that handicap us in our own lives, and whether they are self-inflicted or beyond our control? How is this pigeon symbolic of Calum or the narrator?

Chapter 13 (pp.79-87)

Summary: *More of the lives of the brothers; a story from history told by Grandfather.*

The narrator writes more about his brothers, how, as they grew older, they were drawn farther away from their house by the sea to explore where they could. The overriding impression of these examples is just how poorly the brothers fit in. They are driven to see what they can of the world, but they are ill equipped for taking part in its niceties. They are constantly involved in fights and are forever being stopped by the Royal Canadian Mounted Police for traffic infringements. Something Grandma says about why the three could not come to live with her and Grandpa after their parents' death is applicable: 'but they were too old to be children and still too young to be men' (p.79). They are always in a state of being 'betwixt or between'. Not children, but not men when they were thrust on their own, they are now not quite wild, but not quite civilised. There is no place for them outside their remote Cape Breton house, yet they feel called away from it to places where they can only be 'misfits'. This will be the recurring pattern in their lives.

Grandfather recounts some episodes from the history of the MacDonalds in Scotland. Note how full of ambiguity are his thoughts about his forebears. They were victorious at Killiecrankie in 1692, but they had suffered great losses; they were tired and probably fearful of the future (see BACKGROUND & CONTEXT). Remember, this is the grandfather who lost his father before he was born, and who, as an adult, lost his wife and his only daughter. Grandpa, the jolly one, prefers to think only of the glory and the bravery of the seventeenth-century Highlanders. The difference in their way of viewing clan history speaks of their different approaches to life. Certainly the first grandfather's view is more sophisticated; bravery and vitality are not enough to get through a life that constantly makes you choose between unknowns.

Again we see how the history of the clan is alive in the minds of the current generations. The way they appreciate and define their history in turn defines their character.

Chapter 14 (pp.88-91)

Summary: *The narrator and his sister talk about her trip to Scotland made two years earlier.*

After haunting the outlines of the story like a ghost, the twin sister finally makes an appearance in the narrator's description of a visit he made to her in Calgary two years earlier. She talks about a trip made to Scotland with her husband. She drove around the old lands of the MacDonalds, including Glencoe where many members of the clan were massacred in 1692 (see BACKGROUND & CONTEXT). We are meant to contrast her account of the 'old country' with her very modern home in Calgary and realise that not all exiles take place under conditions of deprivation. The narrator and Catriona share their grandparents' obsession with the past.

Chapter 15 (pp.92-96)

Summary: *An event from the past when the narrator was visiting his brothers is recalled: a pilot whale is beached on the coast.*

The story of the pod of whales (blackfish) swimming near to shore where the brothers live underscores their status as 'children of nature'. They call to the animals and clap and see which one of their songs will get a reaction.

This is the sort of interaction with the natural world, unavailable to city dwellers, which seems to emerge effortlessly out of Calum and his two brothers. This romantic representation of communion between people and animals is shattered by the subsequent beaching of one of the whales, after it comes too close to the shore and tears open its underbelly. It dies slowly, tormented by seagulls. After a violent storm that night, the carcass is washed far inland where it stands 'until only its bones were visible to the eye' (p.96).

Immediately following this image, the narrator refers to his brother waiting in the dingy room while he fetches some alcohol. There is a clear parallel between the whale and the brother. It remains to be seen in what way Calum 'swam too close to land' and ended up with the slow death that the narrator witnesses during these Saturdays in Toronto.

Chapter 16 (pp.97-109)

Key Chapter

Summary: *The narrator's graduation in Halifax (the capital of Nova Scotia) is attended by the three grandparents and his uncle and aunt. On the return trip they discuss the past.*

This chapter gives us some more insight into the characters of the two grandfathers in particular. The occasion is the college graduation of the narrator. His uncle (the father of the other Alexander MacDonald with whom the narrator fights in *Chapter 9*) recalls time spent logging with the narrator's dead father many years before. The serious grandfather (Grandfather) discusses the facts he had looked up at the library in Halifax concerning Wolfe and the Highlanders fighting the French in Canada (see BACKGROUND & CONTEXT). He confirms that Wolfe distrusted the Highlanders and would not have been upset had they all been killed. The phrase he uses gives the book's title; it would be 'No great mischief if they fall' (p.102).

Q Why do you think MacLeod uses this for the novel's title? What does it have to do with the main characters?

Grandfather also reveals the extent to which he is haunted by the loss of his own father before he was born (see CHARACTERS & RELATIONSHIPS). We realise that for these characters the personal past and the past of the greater

clan are inextricably linked. This character's very sense of himself has always been incomplete because he never knew his father. His involvement with his family's history has been some solace but it obviously does not fill all the gaps.

In the course of this discussion, Grandma reads a letter from the relations in San Francisco. It is the time of the Vietnam War and their son, also named Alexander MacDonald, is contemplating going to Canada to avoid the United States draft. This was not uncommon at that time. The grandparents are resolved that the narrator and his brothers shall help him if he comes, for the sake of their common 'blood'.

Soon, jolly Grandpa takes control of the scene; he drinks his whisky and initiates singing among the others to chase away the 'sad stories' (p.107). In his unabashed way he tells of how he gets an erection every time he crosses the water from mainland Nova Scotia to their 'home' of Cape Breton. While this character evidently feels some discomfort when he is not on Cape Breton, he does not share any of the 'misfit' characteristics we associate with Calum or Grandfather or the narrator; in a word, he is not haunted by anything. Like his wife he is inclined to rely on maxims to do his thinking for him without looking too deeply into things. He is an optimist.

Chapter 17 (pp.110-111)

Summary: *Upon returning home, the group finds out that the other Alexander MacDonald, whose parents' car they have been driving, has been killed while mining with the narrator's brothers in Ontario.*

Before the bad news is learned, Grandfather gives the narrator his graduation present, a beautifully carved coat of arms of the MacDonald clan complete with the family motto: 'My hope is constant in thee clan Donald'. It foreshadows the choice the narrator will have to make two chapters later.

Chapter 18 (pp.112-119)

Summary: *The body of Alexander MacDonald is brought back from the uranium mine. On the way from the airport Calum is involved in an incident with the police.*

The narrator drives to the airport, again in his uncle's car, to meet the members of the clan who have accompanied the body back to Nova Scotia. They are drunk and upset, having had to quit their jobs after the managers of the mine refused to let them take time off for the funeral. Calum, driving a rental car, soon outpaces them towards home and is stopped by the RCMP. An incident ensues in which he punches an officer after being hit himself. He and his brothers avoid the pursuing police by driving through backcountry.

Here is another episode in which Calum is associated with blood. His hair is matted with it when they eventually make it back to their grandparents' house (p.115).

Soon police cars arrive with officers looking to arrest Calum. This time Grandma is instrumental in defusing the crisis, asking the officers to leave the family alone in their mourning. The wake and the ensuing funeral proceed without further incident, but the pattern of trouble finding the older brothers, and Calum in particular, continues.

This whole episode shows in many ways the strength of the clan bond. The clan leave the mine as one to attend the funeral; they mourn together; they protect their own against the police.

Chapter 19 (pp.120-122)

Summary: *The narrator decides to take the place of Alexander MacDonald and accompany his brothers and cousins back to the mine.*

After the funeral, the managers of the mine call Calum asking that he return with his clan. They need one more to take the place of the dead Alexander, so the narrator volunteers even though he had won a research fellowship at university for the summer.

Calum spends the rest of the afternoon with his old horse Christy. We are invited to look at his more tender side, reinforcing our image of him as someone more in-tune with nature and animals than with human society.

While the clan derive their strength from their numbers, they tend to follow the will of one leader. In the narrator's generation, Calum is that leader. He assumes this role despite a certain conflict with his nature, which later affects him in very serious ways.

Chapter 20 (pp.123-125)

Summary: *The narrator and the clan return to northern Ontario to resume mining for uranium.*

Renco Development sends cars for the clan as it had promised, driving them up to the site of the uranium mines. Some of the history of mining in the area is given. We should remember the nuclear protesters the narrator sees in present-day Toronto (uranium is a key element in nuclear reactions). One cannot miss the feeling that this mining is done almost 'at the end of the earth', in isolation not only from Cape Breton but from civilisation in general. While the sophisticated mine provides a kind of micro-civilisation of its workers, there will be the feeling about the place that it has laws of its own different from those of the outside world.

Chapter 21 (pp.126-136)

Summary: *An account of daily life at the mine.*

This chapter is very interesting for its depth of detail. The sounds and smells of the mine and the bunkhouses and showers of the mining compound are strongly evoked. MacLeod's gift for detailed writing is most in evidence here, from the feel of the heavy protective clothing to the sounds of the singing coming from the bunkhouse of the French Canadians.

This mining site is something like a 'global village'. Groups of workers from Germany, Portugal, Ireland and other countries have found their way to the compound to carry out some form of labour. It is not just mining that occurs there, though that is obviously the most important function. The members of the clan mostly stick to themselves, as all the other nationalities do; they chat with the Irish about the commonality of their backgrounds, even exchanging their own versions of Gaelic. With the French Canadians however, things will be a little different. The narrator likens them here to the 'opposing team' (p.136) at some kind of sporting event, but we will soon see just how serious the rivalry is between the two groups.

Chapter 22 (pp.137-145)

Summary: *An outsider is smuggled into camp by Calum because he is a MacDonald. An impromptu music session springs up between the clan and the French Canadians.*

Out in the parking lot where non-workers — prostitutes and sellers of black market merchandise — gather, Calum and the narrator come upon a Cree (one of the Native Canadian tribes), named James MacDonald, playing the fiddle. Calum smuggles him into the compound so that he can give James food. Again, the idea of 'looking after your blood' comes to the fore. Though Calum does not technically have any hospitality of his own to offer, he takes it upon himself to extend the conditions of Renco Development to this man with the clan blood in him.

After eating, James MacDonald plays some music on his fiddle for the clan, some of whom join him on their instruments. French Canadian fiddlers soon add to their number. Playing the same old songs with different names both groups soon discover how common their musical heritage is. This scene should be contrasted to one later, in which the two groups will come together under much less friendly terms (*Chapter 37*).

Chapter 23 (pp.146-153)

Summary: *In her house in Calgary the narrator and his sister continue their talk about her trip to Scotland.*

Catriona recalls more details about her trip. This story has a tinge of the supernatural about it. After a night of food and drink with her husband in Aberdeen, she thinks she sees a woman in her bedroom beckoning to her. The woman disappears but the vision deeply affects Catriona. The next day she decides to rent a car and drive to Moidart, the home *Calum Ruadh* left in 1779. A woman recognises her as being of the MacDonald clan and takes her in. They talk about history, and Catriona discovers they cherish the same story about *Calum Ruadh*'s dog. During the time she spends with them, they keep insisting that she has come 'home'.

The significance of this episode is to show how alike all branches of the clan are even after 200 years of separation (present in the group of MacDonalds in Moidart are the ubiquitous black and red hair). They have the same memories, the same stories, the same philosophy.

Chapter 24 (pp.154-156)

Summary: *The narrator continues to ruminate on the difference between the 'pick-your-own' crowd and the imported migrant workers on the farms.*

Chapter 25 (pp.157-159)

Summary: *The narrator reflects the world outside the mine and its compound in that summer of 1968.*

One of the reasons for distrust between the *clann Chalum Ruaidh* and the French Canadians is revealed. The hoistman of the ore-bucket that killed Alexander MacDonald was one of the latter group. The clan wonder if it really was an accident, particularly as the next day the leader of the French Canadians, Fern Picard, tried to get the management of Renco Development to hire some of his own relations to replace the MacDonalds who had left to attend the funeral.

The narrator wonders about life in Halifax, where he turned down his summer research grant:

> At times I missed, or imagined that I missed, the theatres and the restaurants which I hardly ever frequented or the discussions with classmates on the subjects of the day. There was a life, I knew, which was not so totally masculine nor dominated by the singleness of one profession (p.158).

He betrays the measure of difference between himself and the clan. Much as he is attached to them by 'blood', his interests differ from theirs.

Chapter 26 (pp.160-167)

Summary: *An old story about how Grandpa almost drowned on the ice before the death of the narrator's parents is related by one of his brothers in between shifts at the mine.*

This story is interesting in the way it shows Grandpa to have had a sort of 'charmed' life. One of the brothers says, 'It is curious how Grandpa was saved from the ice in March and yet was perceived as a careless man, while our parents who tried to do everything right went down without salvation' (p.167).

It *is* curious. Grandpa was alone and drunk; the only thing that saved him was the good sense of his animals. We do not really know if it is within Grandpa's capacities to realise this. He seems more concerned about whether his 'dick' has been frozen than about anything else. The family is forced by the other grandfather to see the generosity of Grandpa's act; he crossed the ice to bring them hay so their animals would not starve in the long winter.

Chapter 27 (pp.168-176)

Summary: *The narrator returns with beer to Calum in Toronto. They reminisce a while longer before he leaves his brother.*

Having finally chosen some beer, the narrator returns to Calum in his room in Toronto. Calum talks about the past, about the old house and the weather on Cape Breton. He relates another of Grandpa's off-colour jokes, one the narrator had not heard. Calum has lost a lot of the threatening air in his presence, and his talk makes him seem something of a philosopher ('The past is not the same for everyone, but it catches up with you' (p.171)). The alcohol has revived him, at least for a few hours, until he drinks his memories into submission again.

The narrator recalls an anecdote of Grandma's in which Calum as a five-year-old saw himself in Grandpa's beer bottle. Of course it's a grim harbinger of things to come. It seems superfluous. The narrator will soon relate details about the event in Calum's life that really sent him into a downward spiral. Are we not led to believe that this event was responsible for the character's drinking, rather than some predisposition?

As the narrator leaves, the two shake hands. Calum sways and the narrator has to shift his weight to compensate for it: '[w]e lean into one another like two tired boxers in the middle of the ring. Each giving and seeking the support of the other' (p.175). This ties in with the narrator's description of Calum in the first chapter as that of a boxer rocking on the balls of his feet looking for an opening.

Putting the two comparisons together, we see that the meeting with Calum has been something like a boxing match. What the narrator is fighting is the past as embodied in his brother; he is also fighting his guilt.

Chapter 28 (pp.177-180)

Summary: *The narrator continues telling us about his conversation with his sister.*

Catriona reveals more of the way she is drawn to her past and her clan even in far way Calgary. When she is at the airport she will often go to the gates for the flights flying to the East Coast of Canada. What is she hoping to achieve? She does not know, but it is apparent that she cannot break the tie of the clan no matter where she is. Earlier in the chapter she distinguishes between the language of the mind and the language of the heart, implying that English is the former and Gaelic the latter. This highlights again the same division the narrator feels between the old customs of clannish Scotland and the realities of modern Canada.

Chapter 29 (pp.181-183)

Summary: *Another interlude about the migrant pickers of Ontario.*

As he drives home through Ontario, the narrator continues to muse on the migrant field workers he passes, imagining them leaving their work to go home to Jamaica or Mexico, or even to Quebec. He pictures the French Canadians extolling the virtues of their own province over those of Ontario. This draws our attention to the divisiveness among Canadian citizens. Quebec has tried in the past to secede from Canada, and very nearly succeeded, creating some rancour between it and the other Canadian provinces.

Chapter 30 (pp.184-193)

Summary: *Word comes from Grandpa that another Alexander MacDonald, the draft-dodger from San Franciso, is coming to stay with his cousins at the mine.*

The division between Quebec and the rest of Canada, alluded to in the previous chapter, is addressed here in the English lessons the narrator is asked to give Marcel Gingras, one of Fern Picard's French Canadians. They have to be secretive about these lessons, as Picard does not seem to like Gingras associating with the Scotsmen. This is something of a 'Romeo and Juliet' arrangement without the romance (though there are some subtle hints that Gingras may be homosexual). The two discover how similar their languages actually are: 'It seemed, at times, as if Marcel Gingras and I had been inhabitants of different rooms in the same large house for a long, long time' (pp.184-185). This comment can easily be read as an assessment of the larger situation in Canada.

There will be more about this divisiveness as the ill will between the clan and Picard's group is building to a violent confrontation. In this chapter, he and Calum face off with each other momentarily, each going through a certain masculine ritual of spitting on the path (p.190).

More urgently, the American Alexander MacDonald, dodging the draft, is on his way to Sudbury and will have to be picked up. The narrator enlists Calum to help. The latter agrees because it is the right thing to do for his 'blood'. On the journey to Sudbury, they talk about family and history. They discuss the Vietnam War and their father's participation in World War Two. It is important to realise, however, that when the narrator and Calum discuss *the '45* as the war that shaped them, they are not talking about 1945, but 1745 (see BACKGROUND & CONTEXT). This is telling. By bypassing the great, global conflict in which their father fought and naturally settling instead on relatively minor events of 200 years earlier, they show how strongly their identity is shaped by the history of their clan rather than of their country.

Calum reveals something about his sense of guilt and responsibility in his last comment in the chapter. He thinks that if he had been with their parents on that night in March, he might have been able to save them.

Chapter 31 (pp.194-198)

Key Chapter

Summary: *Calum tells the story of a time when he and his two brothers returned from a mining job in Northern Ontario to drill the names of their parents into the rock of the island on which his father was the lighthouse keeper.*

Calum tells the story of the trip back from Ontario during the current trip to Sudbury. It attests to the kind of longing for connection that many people feel when they lose a loved one to a sudden death. The three brothers are haunted by the memory of their parents. The gesture of carving their names on the rock is the only thing they can think of as a tribute to their parents. It is important that they enlist the help of the grandparents. Remember that it was their loss as well. The two generations paying tribute to the lost generation that links them is very poignant.

Their names on the rock face of the island should put us in mind of the boulder marking the grave of the original *Calum Ruadh* (as described in *Chapter 1*). The fresh-water well symbolises the persistence of memory as well as the unbounded sadness in those left behind. The stark remains of their parents' house are also symbolic of the shattered lives of the children who have to continue on without their parents' guidance.

Chapter 32 (pp.199-200)

Summary: *An anecdote told by Calum of their parents and one of Grandpa told by the narrator.*

A rather overwrought symbolic association, that of Grandpa with the male sexual organ, is continued in this chapter. All those off-colour jokes and innuendo are hardly accidental. We might reflect on this: Grandpa is really the only character with any kind of sexuality about him. Though our narrator is married and has children, we never even find out his wife's name, never mind learn anything about their relationship. Sexuality is completely absent in him and the other characters. Perhaps in compensation it overflows in Grandpa until there seem to be few references to this character without some mention being made of his penis (see CHARACTERS & RELATIONSHIPS). There is something peculiar in the way these asexual young men share a story about their grandfather's erection.

Chapter 33 (pp.201-208)

Summary: *Calum and the narrator continue on to Sudbury, pick up the new Alexander MacDonald, and return to the mine.*

On the trip down to Sudbury (which includes a flat tyre as well as Calum being pulled over by the highway patrol), Calum reveals something that has been troubling him. On the day when the other Alexander MacDonald was killed, he had had a fight with Fern Picard. There is indeed a long history of animosity between the two leaders of their respective groups. Calum suspects that Picard had Alexander MacDonald murdered. Calum feels responsible for the death of his cousin, but not just because of the fight. As leader of the clan it was his responsibility to make sure that none of his 'blood' was put into the kind of danger Alexander MacDonald went into unwittingly.

At the airport they immediately recognise the new Alexander MacDonald by his appearance. They take him back to the mine and 'substitute' him for the dead Alexander MacDonald using the latter's old identity card. The narrator comments on the eeriness implicit in such a transaction; of course the mine management couldn't care less which Alexander MacDonald takes his place with the others. This new character shows his personality in a comment he makes to Marcel Gingras concerning the latter's French greeting to the narrator: 'Why don't you speak English? This is North America' (p.206).

Ironically this comment is made just after his cousin Calum has used Gaelic on his way past the security guard — as if it gives him a special pass back into the camp.

Cousin Alexander's question raises several issues. Firstly, is it meant to reveal his character? This is a remarkably provocative comment for a new arrival. Is the new Alexander showing his aggressive nature? He is running from authority and would have every reason not to make waves — on the other hand this truculence may be part of his problem.

Secondly, the sub-text could be that this Alexander identifies first with America and considers Canada as simply an extension of America. But is Alexander's intolerance of Marcel speaking French more than that? Does it indicate his intolerance of other differences, including his own clan roots?

Thirdly, this comment about language also highlights the importance of language as an issue between workers. Language divides the workers into mutually exclusive language groups competing for the upper hand in the mine. It also divides workers. The narrator apparently recognises the inflammatory potential of the American Alexander's remark; he quickly diverts attention from his cousin and defuses the situation by thanking Marcel, in French, for the loan of his car. By interrupting his cousin, the narrator indirectly corrects him. He might also be indicating his surprise at such ignorance, although the cousin is introduced as a person with some education who quotes from a famous Robert Frost poem (p.206).

Q Consider the author's purpose here. In your view, what is the signficance of the newly arrived Alexander's remark to Marcel Gingras? In your response consider whether the author is possibly revealing prejudice against Americans.

Q Consider also the title and line of the Robert Frost poem and its deeper significance for future events.

Chapter 34 (pp.209-222)

Key Chapter

Summary: *The last instalment of the narrator's talk with his sister in Calgary.*

The importance of music

The narrator and his sister continue their discussion, recalling the Scottish legends and Gaelic songs of their childhood. This leads to a discussion of the curative powers of music. The Highlanders sang when going into battle just as the women of the *clann Chalum Ruaidh* sang when they did their washing or stitching together. Song was one of the things that brought the whole clan together, a thing that men as different as Grandfather and Grandpa could share. Soon they are talking about the lonely life and determination of Grandfather, the one who lost his wife and his daughter. They both realise that they are a lot like him in their loss. Back onto music, the sister makes a supercilious comment about the sort of people who 'subscribe to a concert series' (p.212) as she and the narrator do. They are the sort of people who also attend orthodontists. Tried and sentenced in her mind, such people are judged to be rather contemptible compared to those who sit around singing songs in their kitchen.

This thinking leads to a preposterous comparison of the clan with the Zulus of South Africa (based on the fact that they too like to sing) and the Masai of Kenya. She basically sees all proud, musical people as cut from the same cloth. This comparison is preposterous because there is a certain element she is not taking into consideration when she likens the Masai to the Scots. The Scots may have been subject to prejudice and treachery, but as evidenced by their own forebears, they always had somewhere to go, be it Canada, the United States, Australia. The Masai did not have the benefit of a place of refuge from persecution.

Personal and cultural history linked

Talk comes around again to the history of the MacDonalds and the disaster of Culloden and the battle against the French under Wolfe at the Plains of Abraham. We are meant to see again that personal history and cultural history are inextricably linked. Catriona seems to feel as strongly about these battles fought more than 200 years ago as she does about her own family's sad history. She understands Grandfather and his sorrows better by acknowledging the extent to which he too was obsessed with the clan history.

This is evidenced in two illustrations. The narrator relates a story told by Calum of how he and the two other brothers cut a tree one day that would not fall because it was being held up with the other trees by a network of intertwining branches (p.220). Catriona tells how she took a photo of the clan to a photo lab with the intention of having her parents' faces isolated from the group and blown up. It proves impossible. Each story is a little parable of clan living. In the first the surrounding trees holding up the damaged one echoes the kind of support the clan offer when one of their number is stricken; the tree is never yielded — years later it remains standing in its original spot. The second anecdote indicates how the individual cannot be separated from the clan, for better or for worse. And so it is with their memories. The twins cannot remember anything more than the 'idea' of their parents. Whatever they know of their parents is coloured by the recollections of other members of the clan, indeed, by the very faces in the photograph from which they cannot be isolated.

Chapter 35 (pp.223-224)

Summary: *The new Alexander MacDonald settles into life at the mine.*

We find out that this new Alexander is an American Football star, a quarterback (the on-field leader of the team). He is thought of as fearless. It is a measure of his detachment from history that he does not know the Scots lost at Culloden.

Chapter 36 (pp.225-231)

Summary: *An account of other events occurring in North America during that fateful summer of 1968.*

MacLeod raids the *Book of the Year* for 1968 to tell us what was going on in the summer the narrator worked with his brothers in the mine. The new Alexander shows himself to fit in well. Like the narrator and Marcel Gingras, he is more or less immune from the history of 'bad blood' between the *clann Chalum Ruaidh* and Picard's French Canadians. He can even spend time in the bunkhouse of the rival group. Bear this in mind.

Chapter 37 (pp.232-37)

Key Chapter

Summary: *Work is suspended at the mine due to a mechanical failure; the growing tension between the clan and the French Canadians comes to a head with violence.*

Because of the failure of the hoist, all the men find themselves above ground at the one time. The compound is hot and overcrowded. There is nothing to do. Alexander MacDonald buys the clan beer and whisky; one of the members of Picard's group does the same for them. Not long afterwards, Picard begins a fight with Calum. Soon it is an open melee between all the members of the two groups (with the notable exception of the American Alexander MacDonald who is not as fearless as initially portrayed). The narrator finds himself pitted in what could almost be called a life-or-death struggle with a man whose name he does not even know. Calum, being strangled by Picard, manages to get his hand on a wrench that the narrator inadvertently knocks towards him. Swinging it at his opponent, Calum kills him with the blow.

Chapter 38 (pp.238-241)

Summary: *The aftermath of the fight: Calum is charged with second-degree murder and the American Alexander MacDonald flees.*

Because of the violent infractions of his past, Calum is held without bail on charges of second-degree murder. The clan, without their leader, finds themselves as lost as the French Canadians do without Picard. It seems as though everyone will leave the mine. After the fray, the clan break into the foot locker of the American Alexander MacDonald to find that he was a thief; the presence of Fern Picard's wallet shows that the words he had used to start the fight, French for 'thieves' and 'liars', had an element of truth. This Alexander MacDonald did not understand the meaning of 'sticking with your blood'. The words *his* grandmother uses in a letter to thank Grandma and Grandpa are meant to convey a sense of irony.

Chapter 39 (p.242)

Summary: *It is revealed that Calum receives a life sentence for the murder of Fern Picard.*

The theme of Calum as a kind of reincarnation of the old leaders of the MacDonald clan is complete. Leadership never sat comfortably upon him. A bit of a misfit with anyone except his beloved horse Christy, or away from Cape Breton, Calum was nevertheless called upon to lead — first his two younger brothers, and later his generation of the *clann Chalum Ruaidh* — after the death of his parents. And now, like Mac Ian in 1692, he has, in a sense, been sacrificed because of his clan allegiance (see BACKGROUND & CONTEXT).

Chapter 40 (pp.243-244)

Summary: *The later lives of the narrator's two other brothers are described.*

This short chapter may seem tacked-on. The narrator has not even named these two brothers and now dismisses them in a few lines — one 'returns' to British Columbia, the other 'returns' to Scotland. The two who were so close are 12,000 kilometres apart. Is this just the author tying up a couple of minor loose ends — or is it more than that? In fact, several other characters are either not named or almost always referred to by their clan relationship to the author. This lack of names could be a further indication of the overriding importance of the clan and family relationships.

> ***Q*** Is the fact that one brother is immediately led back into the Highland clan relationships important? And while the other flees to British Columbia, who was in the car driving to 'Vancouver or Bust'? Is the dispersal of the two brothers a further statement of the importance of the clan leader and clan structure?

Chapter 41 (pp.245-252)

Summary: *Further wrapping up: the deaths of the narrator's grandparents are discussed.*

Each of the grandfathers dies within character. Grandpa has a coronary attack while trying for the third time to click his heels twice in the air one evening. Grandfather dies quietly in bed after reading a book about Scottish history. In this chapter, Grandma comes to life somewhat. Up to this point she had really been little more than a collection of clichés. The narrator relates that she, like *Calum Ruadh* in the 19th century, died in her 111th year. At the end, she no longer recognises the narrator. More curiously, she no longer sees the past as past; she experiences it as the present. Thus she believes she has a son who is currently a lighthouse keeper off Cape Breton, *even as* she has a grandson who is a wealthy orthodontist in Ontario.

This is the culmination of the theme of memory; in a sense, Grandma, in her final senility is just doing what all the characters in this novel do: living in both the past and the present at the same time.

Chapter 42 (pp.253-255)

Summary: *The ride home from Toronto.*

Driving home the narrator thinks about the migrant workers who are in bed for the night, and about the Masai and the Zulus. It is all a bit desultory, but thinking can be like that when one has had the sort of experience he has that afternoon. In the course of these thoughts we learn that his wife's father and two brothers were murdered in eastern Europe around the time of the Second World War (was it by the Nazis or the Soviets?). This addition seems somewhat gratuitous. However, it is brought in to explain why his wife is so understanding about his need to see his brother regularly. 'We never know what lies ahead of us,' she tells him (p.255). The perhaps unexpected bounty of the suggested history MacLeod gives to the wife is that it reminds us that there are people in the world with sadder histories than the narrator's. Frankly, it highlights the degree of self-indulgence in his and his clan's obsessions with the wrongs done to their forebears. Wolfe's 'no great mischief if they fall' is nothing in comparison to Hitler's Final Solution or Stalin's Gulag.

Chapter 43 (pp.256-262)

Summary: *The next winter, the narrator drives his brother Calum back to Nova Scotia to die.*

After receiving a call in the middle of a blizzard in March, the narrator picks Calum up in Toronto for the long ride to Cape Breton. It seems that under the conditions of his parole Calum was not permitted to leave Ontario, otherwise one would assume he would have settled somewhere in Nova Scotia after leaving prison. The point of this ride is fairly apparent: Calum wants to return to Cape Breton to die. They eventually reach Nova Scotia after difficult driving and some final adventures over a Canso causeway flooded by ocean waves.

It is fitting that the sea should encroach so closely on Calum's final pilgrimage — it has played such a large part in the life of his family — as it is also somehow fitting that they should be pulled over by the police one last time. His problems with authority dog him until the end. As Calum's life ebbs away, the narrator looks at his homeland and is flooded with memories; among them that of the pilot whale that beached on the shore. Once again the parallels to Calum are evident. By the time they come in sight of the lighthouse, with its fresh-water well still pumping, Calum is dead.

CHARACTERS & RELATIONSHIPS

Though there are many characters in this novel, four of them — the narrator, Calum, Grandpa and Grandfather — should be considered the *main characters*. They group themselves fairly naturally in pairs divided along generation lines; Grandpa and Grandfather make one pair, and the narrator and Calum make the other. There are similarities beyond the accident of time. In each of the generations, there is a lucky character and an unlucky character, one thinker and one 'doer', one obsessed by clan history and one busy looking after his family.

The Narrator, Alexander MacDonald (the 'gille beag ruadh'*)*

Key Quotes

'I try to square my shoulders in the September sun — as if I were auditioning for the part of 'twentieth-century man' in a soon-to-be-released spectacular' (p.15).

'My parents were not found that day, or the next, or in the days or months that followed' (p.47).

'This is the story of how my sister and I, as three-year-old children, planned to spend the night with our grandparents and remained instead for sixteen years...This is a story of lives which turned out differently than was intended' (p.52).

'When you throw things away, I suppose, you can never be sure that they will ever be yours again' (p.125).

'We viewed [the French Canadians], as they did us, with a certain wariness; always on the lookout for the real or imagined slight or advantage' (p.158).

'At times I missed, or imagined that I missed, the theatres and the restaurants which I hardly ever frequented or the discussions with classmates on the subjects of the day. There was a life, I knew, which was not so totally masculine nor dominated by the singleness of one profession' (p.158).

'My hands have grown soft from the years exploring the insides of other people's mouths' (p.169).

'Wars touch all of us in different ways...We are probably what we are because of the '45' (p.192).

'[The French Canadians] had lost their leader. We had lost ours' (p.240).

The narrator is a middle-aged, prosperous orthodontist. This is his story, of course, but like many novelistic narrators, he is more an observer than a participant in the events of the novel. He is trying to write about the rather sad history of his family, particularly the story of his oldest brother Calum. Along the way he cannot help revealing things about himself. He is not a particularly happy person despite his prosperity and his stable family life (we learn next to nothing about his wife and children, but we have no reason to think they are *domestically* unhappy). Along with nearly every other character in this novel, the narrator is haunted by his past. One of the *clann Chalum Ruaidh* of Cape Breton, Nova Scotia, he is obsessed by the history of the MacDonalds both in Canada and in Scotland. His maternal grandfather (Grandfather) taught him and his twin sister (Catriona, or Catherine) about Scottish history.

However, clan history intertwines with personal history. One of the reasons might be that the traditional ways of the clan are being lost. It is not insignificant that where very few of the previous generation left Cape Breton, *all* of the surviving children in the narrator's family eventually settle elsewhere. He practises in Ontario, and his sister lives with her family in far away Calgary. The narrator keeps mentioning the importance of extended family. He is very nostalgic about a time when he was living in the 'ancestral' land of Cape Breton where almost everyone he came into contact with was part of the clan. Now, in modern Ontario, he obviously feels isolated.

Relationship between Alexander and Calum

The central relationship in *No Great Mischief* — between the narrator and his oldest brother, Calum — symbolises the extent to which clan living and clan identity has been lost or degraded at the end of the 20th century. The narrator's only role in helping his brother, who is in an advanced stage of alcoholism, is to visit him occasionally on weekends, to give him some alcohol, and eventually to return him to Cape Breton to die. Calum's unhappy history, more than the narrator's indifference, is to blame for this being the extent of their relationship. Still, there is an enormous difference between his sad trips to Toronto and the kind of universal support he and his siblings received when they lost their parents. There is an obvious, if unspoken, layer of guilt in his relationship with Calum. It is also marked by an element of fear, right up to the end.

What really marks the relationship between the narrator and his three brothers is the vast difference in how their lives turned out. His brothers had to look out for themselves and make their lives as best they could, while the narrator and his sister were given everything by their grandparents. The children could be said to have all started out equal; the narrator progresses to a level of comfort and achievement that might have been impossible if his parents had lived, while Calum regresses into a much harder life than he would perhaps have had.

The resulting feelings of guilt in the narrator account for his associating his professional achievements with shame. Orthodontics is promoted as a racket for making riches out of his patients' weakness, their vanity. This guilt is also behind his continuing reference in the novel to the migrant workers of Ontario, as compared to the weekenders picking fruit for themselves. The former group, struggling for their existence like his brothers, is deemed far superior to the weekenders who, like him, act out of their own selfishness.

The professions of the narrator and Calum highlight the difference between the two men and the narrator's sense of shame and inferiority. Calum is a great miner; under strained and dangerous circumstances, he is a true professional as well as a leader of men. The narrator sees himself as a glorified beautician, a leech feeding off the insecurities of others. This position is absurd, of course; he mentions, but downplays the fact that some of his work helps people with painful and debilitating problems. In the chapters concerning the narrator's summer spent at the uranium mine, these differences come into the light. The pressures of the mine, with its extreme heat or cold; its gruelling labour; the tensions between the workers of differing nationalities; the terrible danger of the work — these are all meant to be contrasted with the narrator's consulting rooms decorated in soft browns, a place where no one ever raises their voice. He does the best he can, but by the end of his stay there he is thinking of his lab and his microscope. This seems only natural, but unfortunately the narrator seems to associate his discomfort with a lack of masculinity.

The condition of being 'in-between' — of being pulled equally by the past and by the present; by family loyalty and independence; by his cultural identity (as a descendant

of the Highlanders) and by 'modern Canada' — is really the defining feature of this character.

Calum

Key Quotes

'Ah, poor Christy. How she always kept her part of the bargain' (p.9).

'"Always look after your own blood," Grandma said...I suppose that's why you're here' (p.12).

'The past is not the same for everyone, but it catches up with you' (p.171).

'After our parents died we could not have looked after our sister and you. We could hardly look after ourselves, and...we could not have survived without the help of all those people who brought us chains and saws and a boat and horses' (p.189).

'I look at it differently...If I had been with them [his parents] I might have saved them' (p.193).

Inability to fit in

Calum's defining feature is probably that he does not really fit anywhere in the world, with the possible exception of the old family house on Cape Breton. One of the assumptions we have to make about Nova Scotia is that the opportunities for finding work are scarce. In the earlier generations, Grandpa was very fortunate to get his job maintaining the local hospital, and Calum's father was lucky to get his job at the lighthouse, but it seems as though opportunity has dried up for the latter generation. Calum is very capable and competent; he is described by Marcel Gingras as the best miner he has ever seen (p.173). When Renco Development needs the best man for a delicate dynamiting job in British Columbia, it is Calum they choose. Calum does all the negotiating for the clan. He has always been in charge, ever since his parents died when he was aged 16. The narrator tends to write about the three brothers as a group. But it is obvious that Calum was responsible for the two others and took the role of leader.

There is a well-known quote from Shakespeare's *Henry IV, part II* 'uneasy lies the head that wears a crown'. Calum must lead, but he is really much happier being by himself or with his beloved horse, Christy. He laments that his father died before he was able to teach him what it takes to be a man.

There is something unripe about Calum, and this is the source of his inability to 'fit in'. He has a history of trouble with the law; indeed, he is pulled over by the Royal Canadian Mounted Police no fewer than three times in the course of the novel. On two of these occasions, it just *happens* that Calum is behind the wheel rather than the narrator. This speaks of a certain bad luck Calum has in comparison to his brother. He and his sister had the good fortune to be young enough to be looked after by his grandparents; Calum had to go out on his own when their parents died. The narrator was left alone to pursue his studies and interests while Calum had to go to work and look after his other brothers and a whole battery of cousins following him.

Calum as leader

In a sense, Calum is a kind of scapegoat, in the true meaning of the term; he takes upon himself all the troubles so that the rest of his flock might be untouched. This is why he feels the death of the 'red-haired' Alexander MacDonald so strongly. He likens it to the nail in his shoe from one of Grandma's old sayings: 'you can get used to anything except a nail in your shoe'. Calum is the modern incarnation of the old clan chiefs of MacDonald. There is very little glory in a position like that, but much responsibility and trouble. As some of the old chiefs were sacrificed to treachery, Calum is sacrificed to his sense of responsibility. It is his status as leader that gains him the enmity of Fern Picard. Remember, their fatal brawl begins after a member of the clan betrays them all by stealing and lying; Calum pays the price for this with the blood on his hands and the term in prison which destroys his life.

Calum is more interested in his personal past than he is in the history of the clan. But he is obsessed with the loss of his father. Calum knows that had this event not occurred, he would not have been made to wear the crown. We should notice Calum's 'natural' side in his relations with Christy and in his deep interest in the animals and landscape of his home. Again, one feels that he might have had a happy life pursuing these interests if things had gone differently. We are meant to see the ironic division between his natural calling on the wide open shores of Cape Breton and the life that he ends up in — deep inside the earth as a miner or locked away in prison.

A tragic figure

Calum is a tragic figure because of all these things. He is the 'unlucky' brother sacrificed to the hard ways of the past and to the family responsibilities of clan living. This might be the significance of his seeming always to be covered in blood. The narrator is the 'lucky' brother, the one who escapes the responsibility, but is forever haunted by the past and by his guilt about the fate of the other.

Grandpa

Key Quotes

'I know *one thing* really well and that's how to run this hospital. That's enough for me' (p.34).

'Poor *'ille bhig ruaidh*...Things will never, ever again be the same for you' (p.48).

'I believe I'll have another beer. We're not here for a long time but for a good time' (p.64).

'My hope is constant in thee, Clan Donald' (p.82).

'No more sad stories...Let's sing some songs' (p.107).

The narrator's paternal grandfather, he and Grandma raise the twins from the age of three after the accident occurs. We are encouraged to think of the two grandfathers together in this novel. One is hardly ever mentioned without the other being around. They are best friends, but of course they are complete opposites.

Grandpa is jolly, outgoing, vivacious. He is not a shining light of intelligence, but he has a kind of earthy wisdom. When questions arise that have any tinge of philosophy or metaphysics, he tends to offer a bawdy story or a crude joke (at one point the other Grandfather calls him a smart man who should think more). This does not mean that such a response does not address the question in its way. He is a homespun philosopher, sentimental and emotional. He drinks enough that it would be a problem in many people, but it does not seem to be a problem with him. Contrast Grandpa's drinking with Calum's. He does not become a slave to alcohol as his grandson does, nor does it separate Grandpa from his family. This is mostly due to the understanding nature of his wife, but then Grandpa never seems to be anything other than a 'jolly' drunk (heavy drinking rarely works this way).

Grandpa is very lucky. Helped by Grandfather, he gets the right job at the right time. He and Grandma call it 'the chance'. After that, they know they'll be set for life. Remember Grandpa's incident with the ice. Drunk and alone and on a horse-driven cart, Grandpa miraculously avoids falling through the broken ice. Otherwise able to laugh about everything, he never again mentions the incident after his son, daughter-in-law and grandchild are killed under similar circumstances — but while taking every possible precaution. His good luck should be contrasted not just to the bad luck of those killed, or to Calum's, but to the bad fortune of the other grandfather. Again, there seems to be a lucky one and an unlucky one in each generation, just as there are black-haired MacDonalds and red-haired MacDonalds.

But Grandpa is more than a bumbling old fool. He leads when necessary, and he looks after his family. He is generous. Remember that he was on a mission to bring hay to his son's animals on the night he almost fell through the ice (we might remember too that it was his animals, the horse and the dog, who saved him on that night). Like Calum he seems to have a natural affinity with animals (not shared by the narrator, for instance, who does not even have a dog in his fancy house). He mourns the death of his son's dog, shot by the new lighthouse keeper from Pictou.

Perhaps the most conspicuous thing about this character is his sexuality. He does not just make bawdy jokes. He constantly refers to the male reproductive organ. Of course this goes with his 'earthiness', but sometimes the author seems to be laying it on a bit thick. There is a definite distinction in this novel between the body and the mind. The old days of Scotland and Cape Breton are aligned with the former, as the older generations are admired either for their great capacities for fighting or hard work. Then there are the thinkers, like the narrator and his sister, who are obsessed with the past but detached from it because they do not take part in such physical activities.

A 'doer', like Grandpa, attributes his own traits (vitality, bravery, good humour) to the mysterious figures of the past — like Calum Ruadh *or the Highlanders who fought at Killiecrankie and Culloden Moor — while a 'thinker' like Grandfather attributes to them contemplation and worry.*

Grandpa, a man who enjoys drink and sex and other physical vocations, a worker and not a thinker, represents the 'body'. The rather weak conclusion to all this thinking is that in the narrator's mind the old ways are *masculine*, while the new ways are somehow *feminine*. There is something of this in the narrator's sense of shame about his orthodontist practice, his expensive clothes and his delicate fingers. He sees himself as less virile than the previous generations, and along with him seem to be included the rest of us who live in the modern world. I believe this is why Grandpa — who is the most persistent symbol of the 'old way' in his life — has such a pronounced sexuality.

Grandfather

Key Quotes

'[*Calum Ruadh*] was...crying for his history. He had left his country and lost his wife and spoke a foreign language. He had left as a husband and arrived as a widower and a grandfather, and he was responsible for all those people clustered around him. He was...like the goose who points the V, and he temporarily wavered and lost his courage' (p.22).

Grandma 'We have suffered a great loss, but we have other children and we have each other...Nobody knows the depths of [Grandfather's] sorrows' (p.50).

'Still MacDonald died fighting *for* the British Army, not *against* it. And one doesn't like to think of people giving their best, even their lives, under deceptive circumstance' (p.102).

'I have never gotten over that...Not knowing whether my father ever knew that he might be responsible for me, or someone like me. I think it would have made a difference' (p.106).

Grandpa and Grandfather

The other grandfather is a contrast to Grandpa in almost every way. He is neat, fastidious and precise. Think of the difference in their professions. Grandpa does general maintenance; it is no doubt complicated, but a job composed of many small uncomplicated jobs. Grandfather is a carpenter, used to doing complex, finely tuned work in which there is no room for error. In contrast to Grandpa's large family and long and happy marriage, Grandfather loses his wife (giving birth to their daughter) after only one year of marriage. After the death of his wife, Grandfather resolves to be both mother and father to his child. He cooks for her and cleans house; he braids her hair and makes her look as pretty as any mother could. There is a universality about this character, as though he were really able to do anything he sets his mind to. (Grandpa, in contrast, brings home his pay cheque and leaves everything else up to Grandma.)

Grandfather's isolation

While both grandfathers are MacDonalds, Grandfather is about the only character from his generation, or the ones following it, to feel isolated because of his 'blood'. This is due to his being born out of wedlock, fathered by a man who was killed in the woods of Maine before Grandfather was ever born. He himself was a constant reminder to his mother of her shame, and it is suggested that she used to take it out on him. The circumstances of his birth haunt this character throughout his life, not because he shares his mother's shame, but because he never knew his father. This may be why he is so capable — because he had to teach himself everything (in this there is an interesting comparison to Calum); still he implies that the void left by his father has been great indeed. Again, it is from him that the narrator and his sister 'got' their sense of history (almost like the way they 'got' their red or black hair).

With Grandfather, as with the twins, one senses that the desire for history is a manifestation of his desire for a father.

In contrast to Grandpa's sexuality is Grandfather's almost total lack of it. This extends beyond his dislike of off-colour jokes. Grandfather was married for less than a year and widowed at a pretty young age. He is never engaged in any kind of romantic association after that. This and his dislike of any talk about sex (he even has to bring his daughter to Grandma when it is time for her to learn about menstruation) make him seem something like a monk. He is allocated to the 'mind' rather than the 'body'.

Return to heritage

In Grandfather's scholarliness, there is a sense not so much that he is moving away from the 'old ways' of fighting and loving etc., but that the multiple tragedies in his life have forced a life of contemplation upon him. One must have a pretty strong philosophy to face as much loss as he has without caving into it (remember, he has lost his father, his wife and his only child). Grandfather's love of history and his immersion in his culture are a source of strength for him. Nothing illustrates this better than the story of him going out to the lighthouse to take over the duties of his dead son-in-law (*Chapter 7*). Alone on the island, he plays his beautiful Scottish songs all night. He does not seem to be seeking consolation so much as trying to find a foundation upon which to start over in the face of a repeat visit from devastating grief. Some people turn to religion in times of strife; this character turns to his heritage, and his immersion in it is clearly the source of the strength that makes Grandma call him a 'rock'.

Grandfather is a more complicated character than Grandpa, but neither one of them is really a complete person. Grandpa lacks Grandfather's philosophy and introspection, but he has a *joie de vivre* and a flexibility that Grandfather lacks. While these two characters are fully drawn, they are basically two halves of a separated whole. This quality sometimes makes them seem like vehicles for a point the author is trying to make, rather than real people.

What would this point be? Well, clearly the narrator is a lot more like Grandfather than he is like Grandpa — in fact he shares almost none of the latter's traits. Though he obviously respects Grandfather, the narrator tends to devalue that character's characteristics as they are manifested in himself. He would like to be more like Grandpa. Much of the narrator's story is about the way he cannot really fit in either, though he is not a misfit in the same way Calum is. He is unbalanced because he has too much of the one grandfather and not enough of the other. Indeed the only character in this novel who really does 'fit in' is Grandpa. At the narrator's graduation at Halifax, Grandfather goes off to the university library to look up something about James Wolfe while Grandpa goes off to find himself a tavern. To each his own diversions; but while Grandfather finds something to trouble his thoughts, there can be little doubt that Grandpa fitted right in at his destination, trading stories with the barflies and making friends all around.

Other characters

Note: While both Grandma and Catriona play large parts in the novel, they are rather one-dimensional.

Grandma

Key Quotes

'[T]here are some things I really believe in. I believe you should always look after your blood. If I did not believe that...where would you two be?' (p.53).

'A lot has happened to us on this day...but we will have to face this. We will have to be strong. We can't dissolve like a spoonful of sugar in a glass of water' (p.111).

'Blood is thicker than water' (p.187).

'Although [Grandpa and Grandfather] were so different they were each other's closest friend. Throughout their lives, they were each a balance to the other' (p.245).

'All of us are better when we're loved' (p.250).

Until her final appearance, when in her senility, she unwittingly comes to symbolise the conflict between the present and the past inherent in all of the clan (see CHAPTER-BY-CHAPTER ANALYSIS), Grandma is rather straightforward. She defines her life on a set of old clichés and maxims: 'a penny saved is a penny earned', 'blood is thicker than water', 'you can get used to anything, except a nail in your shoe'. There are two occasions when she seems to break out of this program — when she diffuses the dangerous scene at the wake of Alexander MacDonald by asking the RCMP patrollers to respect their mourning (*Chapter 18*); and when at the very beginning of the novel she mourns over all the tomatoes being ploughed into the fields outside of Leamington (*Chapter 1*). The narrator and Catriona obviously have a deep affection for her, and she is a very admirable character for truly following her maxim ('look after your blood') by taking care of her orphaned grandchildren. She is very caring and understanding, particularly in the matter of her husband's drinking. They are a perfect match for each other and an excellent model for their grandchildren. However, because we really know nothing about the later domestic lives of the twins, we cannot see much of this influence at play.

Catriona

Key Quotes

'[A]nd then I began to speak to her and to them in Gaelic...I don't even remember what I said, the actual words or the phrases. It was just like it poured out of me, like some subterranean river that had been running deep within me and suddenly burst forth' (p.150).

'Do you ever think about that, about the way you speak, about the language of the heart and the language of the head?' (p.178)

'Perhaps that's why [Grandfather] became so interested in history...He felt that if you read everything and put the pieces all together the real truth would emerge...Perhaps he felt that if he couldn't understand his immediate past, he would try to understand his distant past' (pp. 215-216).

This character is perhaps the one most obsessed with the past. Unfortunately, there is very little else to her. While some stories are told about her when she was a child, like the time she coloured her hair, the narrator really seems to *know* very little. This is most peculiar in a twin-relationship. Nearly all of her input takes place through a recalled conversation in her expensive home in Calgary two years before. She talks about her trip to Scotland with her husband, and how she went to visit the old MacDonald lands. It is assumed that her interest in the past is heightened by the fact that she has settled so far away from Cape Breton. In revealing how she often goes to the gates loading the flights for the east coast when she is at the airport, she shows herself to feel dislocated by this move and detached from her homeland. She knows a lot more about the history of the clan than the narrator does.

There is something artificial in the conversation between the two characters. Talking to each other as though interviewing for a job, there is none of the naturalness one would assume between siblings, never mind twins (there is some of this in the style of conversation between Calum and the narrator as well, but the difficulty of their history together explains this). Often they seem to slip into exactly the same kind of impersonal talk; this is most unconvincing when one of the characters (usually Catriona) tells the other something he or she would *already know*. MacLeod is more uncomfortable with this character than any other. She has been deemed necessary for explaining things to the reader, about the past and about their life as children, but she seems created *only* for that purpose. She really does not have a life of her own as do Calum and Grandpa and Grandfather.

THEMES & ISSUES

Clan Loyalty and Family Love

Perhaps the most persistent comment made by the members of *clann Chalum Ruaidh* is Grandma's 'look after your blood', or some variation of it. As a statement, it is something of a platitude, but this novel explores in depth how complicated can be the call of one's blood and history. The theme begins in the very first chapter when Calum challenges the narrator by referring to Grandma's maxim and saying, 'I suppose that's why you're here?' (p.12). The narrator is nonplussed; his inability to respond one way or the other indicates just how complicated the issue is. Why should this be? After all, is he not there for that very reason? But to say so would be to throw a wall between them. Calum and the narrator shelter the American Alexander MacDonald (whom they have never even met) because of 'blood'. Surely there should be a stronger reason than that for the narrator coming to support his own brother.

The narrator's dilemma indicates that there is something divisive about all this blood loyalty. It is the cement that keeps the clan together, but it does not necessarily work the same way within immediate families. Think of the narrator and the red-haired Alexander MacDonald fighting over which of them is the 'real' grandson to Grandpa; what they are fighting for is possession of an exclusive love, one that goes beyond the loyalty to the clan (*Chapter 9*). Grandpa is not really able to satisfy either child, just as the narrator is unable to show that his feelings for his brother go beyond clan loyalty in this first chapter. One suspects that this inability is really why he needs to write the book in the first place, to understand his feelings for his brother and isolate them against his general feelings of clan loyalty. Only by measuring the two types of affection can he really understand himself. The end of the novel also signals the end of this philosophical investigation. His statement, 'all of us are better when we're loved', and his reaching for the hand of his brother (in much the same way he and his twin sister automatically reach for the other's hand), suggest that he has come to realise that his feelings for his brother are based on family love rather than mere loyalty.

Let's look at this distinction a bit more closely. Calum and the other two brothers owe their initial survival after the deaths of their parents to the loyalty of the MacDonald clan. But it can give them a start only; the three have to become men on their own. The narrator and Catriona, however, are basically given new 'parents' and all the benefits of their love and guidance. This is another of the things distinguishing the two groups of siblings; where Calum and the others only have 'the clan', the narrator and Catriona have a 'family'. MacLeod is telling us that there is a considerable difference. The influence of his three grandparents on the life of the narrator is immeasurable, while the *absence* of parental guidance in Calum's life is the strongest reason for his being unable to interact successfully in the world outside.

Clan ties are very strong; Calum takes the responsibility of his generation onto his own shoulders — probably as a way of repaying the debt he owes to the clan. But notice how isolating it is. Though Calum is a very capable leader, it clearly goes against his introspective nature; though always surrounded by clan, he really seems to be a loner. When the Ontario judge asks him if he needs a lawyer, Calum responds, 'I have been looking after myself since I was sixteen…I can handle this' (p.239). This is not an answer any of his siblings would have given. In assuming leadership, Calum has had to grow up fast and in ways perhaps unnatural to him — to become the bearer of burdens. Clan loyalty is one of those burdens, no matter how strongly he believes in it.

It is also indirectly responsible for his undoing. The brewing animosity between Calum and Fern Picard finally boils over into violence because of the American Alexander MacDonald's betrayal of this loyalty. The diaspora of the Highland clans, which to a large extent was forced in the 'Clearings' of the 19th century, sent clan members all over the globe. What has made such a trauma a little easier to take is the sense of kinship and heritage these clans have continued to share despite the intervention of so many miles and years. It is present in *No Great Mischief* in the sense of loyalty Grandma and Grandpa share with their relations in San Francisco, despite not having seen them for so many years. The American Alexander MacDonald's betrayal thus goes beyond merely letting his cousins down; he turns his back on the most important part of his heritage, the thing that has bound the MacDonalds together after the loss of their homeland and their dispersal.

The important thing to consider with the theme of clan loyalty and family love is this. Both Calum and the narrator start out with the same circumstance. They lose both parents early in life. Being too young to look after themselves, the narrator and his sister find a family situation to replace the one they lost. Having such a foundation, it is up to them afterwards to determine how much clan loyalty they will extend or accept. Calum, forced to make his own way, is denied such family love and support. He and the other brothers have only each other; they stick together, but somehow they are more like a 'clan-within-the-clan' than a family. Being the leader, the burden and the isolation fall most heavily on Calum. *All* he has in the future is clan loyalty — he cannot choose whether he will provide it or accept it any more than he can transform clan loyalty into the family love he has lost. Nothing is said about the way the two other brothers feel about Calum and nothing is said about Catriona's feelings for him; all we can go on is what the narrator tells us about his own feelings.

The source of the narrator's undeniable, if somewhat suppressed, feelings of guilt concerning his brother is that he never extended anything beyond clan loyalty towards him. In the interim between his going to see Calum in the boarding house in Toronto and his final ride with him to Cape Breton six months later (in other words, in the narrative space filled by the telling of his 'story'), the narrator appears to realise this. That final journey is a gesture of love succeeding over loyalty.

Ghosts of the Past

A point should be made: the population of Scotland is currently about five million. But tens of millions of people around the world claim Scottish descent. It is a similar story with Ireland; taken together (some call this the 'Celtic Diaspora'), there would be perhaps hundreds of millions of people around the world tracing their heritage back to two tiny countries linked by a commonality of origin with a combined population of fewer than ten million. This may give some indication of why the descendants of the migrant Scottish Highlanders take their heritage so seriously. It is responsible, at least in part, for the continued clan loyalty discussed above, and it plays a role in the kind of obsession with history shared by a number of characters in *No Great Mischief*.

One might be *only* nostalgic for a nation left behind that yet remains the way it was. But when the nation is changed utterly, that sense of loss and nostalgia must be increased exponentially. The urgency of Grandfather's study of the past is that of a man trying to hang on to a life already lost.

That is also the case with modern day Nova Scotia. As Grandfather rhapsodises on the Highlander past, the narrator does the same regarding the 'old ways' of the *clann Chalum Ruaidh* on Cape Breton. There has been an exodus from the 'new' ancestral homeland too, a second diaspora due to a lack of opportunity. In a sense, the narrator's generation is forced to do what *Calum Ruadh* and his heirs found impossible — to leave the old country truly behind and become 'Canadians', mentally as well as physically. It is not necessarily a welcome adjustment. In *No Great Mischief* events tend to repeat themselves over succeeding generations. We should recognise how the narrator and his sister and brothers are 'reliving' the immigration of *Calum Ruadh* in their separation from their Cape Breton heritage. Cape Breton is their 'old country', their lost homeland. The central conflict in Calum's life stems from his having to weather the necessary changes of living away from Cape Breton without being properly equipped to do so.

It is this separation that makes the narrator and Catriona so interested in clan history as well. As the first generations of immigrants held so strongly to their culture in the New World, this first generation to leave Cape Breton *returns* to its roots as a way of navigating the course of their lives. As with most people trying to figure out who they are, their first step is to understand who they *were*. By the end of the novel, we cannot conclude whether the narrator really understands his past or his present — though his reconciliation with Calum indicates a positive step. What is important is that for all his success and his cynical pronouncements on modern life, this novel finds him in very much the same position as the newly landed *Calum Ruadh* 'crying for his history' and temporarily 'losing his way'.

Loss of Parents and Individual Identity

Calum Ruadh leaves his past beyond the sea; in the case of his wife, who died on the voyage, one could say his past is left *in* the sea. This is also true for the narrator and Calum (and the rest of the children). The drowning of their parents does indeed repeat the first *Calum Ruadh*'s loss of his wife, and it is the most important factor in separating the children from their Cape Breton upbringing. All of us can think of our past as something submerged within our memories or consciousness. For the narrator and his siblings that notion has its truth in reality; their past is their parents and it has been drowned. The Highlander heritage we have been discussing is nothing more than a connection forged between individuals who look the same way at a shared past. When their parents slip under the ice with their brother Colin, the bond these characters have to their past is broken. The way that Calum, the narrator and Catriona go about trying to forge that bond again is perhaps the most important aspect of their individual identities, and it is what the novel is about.

For Calum it means taking on the role of clan leader. In this we really get to see how the past is repeated. The 'goose who makes the V', Calum is a bit like *Calum Ruadh*, a bit like the betrayed Mac Ian of Glencoe. He is also like those Highlanders defeated so badly on Culloden Moor who must have known that their way of life was coming to an end, even if they were victorious. Though the characters in the novel would surely deny it, Calum may even be a bit like James Wolfe. To Grandfather and Catriona, Wolfe symbolises treachery (definitely not a characteristic shared by Calum), but are we sure this is Alistair MacLeod's opinion?

Past and Present Struggles

In the section BACKGROUND & ISSUES I discuss the relationship between Wolfe and the Highlanders. His 'no great mischief' comment seems awfully cavalier, but surely there is room to understand a man commanding troops *against* whom he had battled only 14 years earlier. I mentioned above how the narrator's generation is the first to go out and become fully assimilated Canadians. Consider the political climate in Canada today. The most difficult issue is the question of secession by Quebec. The referendum on it a few years ago, which very nearly passed, has brought to a head the tensions between French Canada and English Canada present ever since Wolfe's time. In a sense, the struggle between the two Canadas is a battle for the 'soul' of modern Canada. With this in mind we can see how the fight between the *clann Chalum Ruaidh* and Fern Picard's men symbolically plays out this continuing struggle, as it repeats in its way the battle at the Plains of Abraham. You'll recall that in that battle both leaders, Wolfe and Montcalm, were killed, just as in the fight Picard is killed and Calum's life is effectively ended. As the narrator writes, 'They had lost their leader. We had lost ours' (p.240). The key elements for Grandfather concerning the battle of the Plains of Abraham, namely loyalty and treachery and the ambiguities of leadership, are all present in this fight at the mine. The past is replayed, not just in the way Calum stands up for (and is sacrificed to) clan loyalty like the leaders of old; the fight also replays the epic struggle for Canada in the 1750s, one that does not want to end. The ghosts of the past never really go away.

Animal Imagery and the Natural World

MacLeod's use of natural metaphors and animal imagery is an element of his style, but it also has thematic relevance. Think of the *clann Chalum Ruaidh* dogs. These dogs are practically characters in the novel, or better said, *one* character, present throughout the years. Obviously many generations of dogs come and go, but they all have the same characteristics of fierce loyalty and devotion. It is a clan truism that 'it was in those dogs to try too hard'. The dog killed by the man from Pictou is in a sense the *same* dog which swims out to *Calum Ruadh* 170 years earlier.

The constancy and interchangeability of the dogs mirrors the qualities in the human members of the branch. As Calum is destroyed by his loyalty to the clan, so too the family dog dies for caring too much; and as the latest generations of clan dogs are carbon copies of their eighteenth-century matriarch, so too Calum is a twentieth-century reincarnation of Mac Ian.

Old Values and the Natural World

However, there is another element to these symbolic equations. MacLeod is implying that the old ways of the clan are much more 'natural' than modern ways. It is not just that the clan used to 'live close to the land'; we are being asked to make an association between the old values of loyalty, hard work and bravery, and the workings of the natural world. This is done in more ways than just likening the clan to their dogs (it should be remembered to what extent dogs, domesticated animals, have been removed from the 'natural' world). It is also done through some of the images already mentioned, like the goose that makes the 'V' during migration, the pilot whale which swims too close to land, beaches and dies, even the well-spring of sweet water on the island off Cape Breton.

Each of these is somehow related to Calum, of course, but only to those aspects of Calum's personality which interact with the accepted ways of the clan. Calum's affinity with animals, or at least with the horse Christy, is another indication of his closer position to nature. He always says about her that she kept her part of the bargain. This refers to his giving her oats when she pulls the brothers' boat out of the water, but it alludes to his philosophy at large concerning loyalty and the correct way of doing things. In a still larger context, it seems to have something to do with the human place in nature. Nature does not work in half-measures; it does not manipulate or dissemble. Like Christy it is completely honest and dependable. To Calum this is what a man should be.

The kind of honesty that comes naturally to horses and dogs is extraordinarily hard for humans. Something in human interactions is always conspiring against achieving it. Remember how angry Calum is the time his brother forgets the oats for Christy. Not keeping his part of the bargain, even once, is a kind of debasement for Calum; its dishonesty drives a wedge between him and the natural order, and the man he aspires to be. This is perhaps the greatest source of his burden as clan leader, to attain the kind of sincerity and integrity of Christy or *Calum Ruadh*'s dogs in the complex human realm of Elliott Lake and elsewhere. Calum seems to sense that, due to their being immune to human inconsistencies, these animals are the 'true' keepers of the ancient clan ways.

The other character in this novel with an extraordinary affinity for animals is Grandpa. While Grandpa is not necessarily more loyal than Grandfather, for example, he is certainly less complicated. Like Christy or the clan dogs, Grandpa does not have to think about what is right; he is untroubled by doubt. Grandpa is also the character who most strongly represents the 'ways of the past', the clan traditions that are more along the course of nature. The narrator's comment that '…'the lamp of the poor' is hardly visible in urban southwestern Ontario…And the stars are seldom clearly seen above the pollution of prosperity' (p.176) indicates how MacLeod aligns modernity with the unnatural.

What is 'natural' and what is not

Again, it is significant that the narrator does not even have a dog after all his exposure to animals in his childhood. It shows to what extent this 'twentieth-century man' has moved away from the natural world. He no longer lives on wild Cape Breton; he lives in a gated community in an affluent neighbourhood in Ontario. This issue of what is 'natural' and what is not is complicated when the setting of the novel moves to the mine at Elliot Lake. This very remote location might be called the wilderness, but consider what has been placed there. In the middle of this forest with its moose and stands of pine, is this insular community having nothing to do whatever with the setting (other than destroying it).

The world of the Renco Development mine is about as unnatural as one could imagine; workers live on top of each other in inhospitable quarters, and they work shifts at all hours. Natural time no longer exists at a place where miners come out of the ground after their shift wondering if the sun is still shining or if it is the middle of the night. Being so far underground is terribly unnatural for people. Consider what the use of the uranium they are mining will be; it will go to make the most appalling and unnatural of human creations, nuclear weapons.

Displacement of the Clan

That the *clann Chalum Ruaidh* must seek this kind of work is another indication of how lost they are in this modern world (and rootless: they follow the same kind of work all over the world). Again, things are complicated. Some of the old 'ways' might be present — the loyalty, the fraternity, and the hard work — but the object toward which they are being applied is completely divorced from the life of the past, in a bewildering and hostile environment. The first generation of Highlanders to the New World had a lot to deal with, but the landscape and climate of Cape Breton would have been pretty similar to their home. They would have pursued trades (logging, hunting and fishing) that were at least familiar to them. The succeeding generations would have come to feel bound to Cape Breton just as strongly as their predecessors were bound to the Highlands. For this latest generation, the 'New World' is a mine in South Africa or in Peru; it is an unnatural place like the Renco Development compound at Elliot Lake. In a sense they are reliving the displacement of the original Highlanders; they are landless people. But there is an added element of dislocation. Where the original migrants were able to find a new 'natural' element where they could apply the fundamental abilities they had acquired over thousands of years, the new generation must attach themselves to lives not only unfamiliar, but unnatural.

Language and Identity

The characters in *No Great Mischief* often use Gaelic words or phrases. This use of the 'old' language shows us how language is intertwined with identity. It is important for the main characters as it helps to keep people together, to give them another bond and it gives them a sense of identity. The narrator, for example, in *Chapter 2*, indicates how he has always identified more strongly with his Gaelic name *gille beag ruadhe*, than his given name, Alexander.

- Consider the use of language in establishing personal and clan or group identity.
- Consider also the use of French by the French Canadians and its importance to them.
- How does language unite and divide people?

Family Relationships, Roles, and Individual Identity

While the importance of the clan and family is a major theme, it is also interesting to look at how family relationships are often used as a major way to identify and understand characters – Grandpa, Grandfather, twin sister, the two older brothers (never named), cousin Alexander so on. This suggests the overriding importance of the group – both the family and the clan – but seems to go further. Individual differences between Grandfather and Grandpa, for example, are largely explained by their family histories and how the events affecting immediate family have shaped their lives, characters and personalities. Grandfather lives a lonely, fairly isolated life because of the shame he feels over the circumstances of his illegitimate birth, his father's untimely death and the deaths of his wife and only child. Grandfather is not connected and engaged with others the way Grandpa is. It could be argued that Grandpa's good fortune in having a long and happy marriage and big family play a major role in shaping his personality. These factors give him stability, emotional richness, connectedness with others, fewer personal problems and more straightforward ways of operating.

Alexander MacDonald is firstly identified as the *gille beag ruadh* — the little red-haired boy — something that links him with one side of the clan and distinguishes him from the black-haired members. At first we know him almost entirely in his role of narrator. We only gradually learn, often quite incidentally, about his privileged lifestyle. We get very little insight into his personal struggle because the focus is on the role of family for him and his twin sister — the lucky ones — as compared with Calum and the other brothers who bring themselves up.

- Does the novel suggest that family relationships and family history are the major factors in influencing individuals' identities and life patterns? Consider a wide range of characters.

The Importance of Place

The other factor that can be seen as a major influence on individual lives and their identities is the importance of place. Alexander and Catriona, for example, have moved far from their Cape Breton home in Nova Scotia. Calum lives his life first alone with his brothers in the old clan homestead near the sea and then nomadically moving from mine to mine until he is imprisoned – rather like a displaced person. Scotland remains a place where family welcome people home as if they have never left.

Related to place is the idea of modernity which is more complicated than the simpler existence of lives led in rural areas.

- Explore the idea that closeness to nature leads to more authentic lives than the more artificial life of city dwelling.
- What do you think is the importance of place to individual identity?

QUESTIONS AND ANSWERS

Part 1 Questions

1. 'We are all of us better when we are loved.' This phrase first appears in *Chapter 41*, and is similar to the last line of the book. How are characters affected by love or lack of it in *No Great Mischief?* Consider two or three main characters.
2. The woman in Scotland tells Catriona, 'You are home now' (p.153). Discuss the meaning of home in this context and how this impacts on several characters' lives.
3. 'This is a story of lives which turned out differently than was intended' (p.52). Discuss.
4. 'Living in the past is not living up to our potential' (p.56). How are these words on a woman's shirt in Toronto applicable to the narrator and his family?
5. Grandma, talking about her husband and Grandfather, says, 'Although they were so different they were each other's closest friend. Throughout their lives, they were each a balance to the other' (p.245). Discuss the differences and similarities of the two grandfathers.
6. 'Calum is a tragic character.' Do you agree?
7. In your view does the narrator feel guilty about his privileged life?
8. 'The relationship between Calum and Alexander shows that only duty keeps them in touch with each other.' Do you agree?
9. How does animal symbolism help you to understand Calum and others?
10. 'My Hope is constant in thee, Clan Donald.' What does this quote (attributed to Robert the Bruce at Bannockburn) mean to each of the four characters who use it: Calum (p.175), Grandpa (p.82), Grandfather (p.110) and the narrator (p.90)?

Part 2 Questions

11. What does the part played by the American Alexander MacDonald in the fight between the clan and Fern Picard's men tell us about the role of clan loyalty in modern times?

12. How is the full episode at the Elliot Lake uranium mine applicable to the life of the clan in the outside world?
13. How do the episodes with the migrant fruit pickers illustrate the narrator's general view of the contrast between the 'old ways' and the modern world? Why else might they be included?
14. What does the novel have to say about the importance of family?
15. What part does the Cape Breton locale play on the lives and the identities of the characters in the novel?
16. 'In *No Great Mischief* loyalty to the clan is shown to be as divisive as it is cohesive.' Discuss.
17. This novel deals mostly with the lives of men. Discuss.

Analysing a Sample Question

Part 2, Question 5: What does the novel have to say about the importance of family?

This is a rather general question. *No Great Mischief* is, of course, all about family. Obviously it would be impossible to try to cover everything it has to say. But it is always better to have too much to think about than too little.

The key to writing any essay is getting your information together — to know *what* you are going to write about *before* you start to write. You can do this by making lists or writing down your ideas. This will help to get your thoughts flowing, to clarify your thinking and to choose your main focus so that the topic becomes manageable. By limiting the elements you will write about, you have room to analyse each of them in some depth.

First, think about the main events in the novel that show how family members help each other in times of crisis. Jot these down in a list. Even the quickest survey in your mind would have to highlight the following:

- the drowning of the narrator's parents when he was three;
- the subsequent raising of him and his twin sister by their paternal grandparents;
- the narrator's visiting Calum in Toronto;
- the final ride made by the two of them back to Cape Breton.

Other possibilities:

- Grandfather helping Grandpa get the job at the hospital;

- the narrator taking the place of the red-haired Alexander MacDonald at the mine;
- the fight he has with the same character many years before over the affection of Grandpa;
- Grandfather's loss of his own father — and his wife and daughter.

Next think about the important *relationships* between family members and what they show about family loyalties. Focus on the evidence of relationships which will help you develop the strongest argument.

- *No Great Mischief* is written in the first person; we know a lot more about the narrator than we do about any other character. Obviously you will have more opinions about his relationships than any other character's. I would suggest that the most interesting relationship is between the narrator and his brother Calum.
- Also important are the relationships between him and his twin sister, and between him and his grandparents.
- Don't ignore relationships between other characters completely; the one between the two grandfathers would make an excellent comparison to the relationship of the narrator and Calum.
- Now go to your list of some of the important events. Save the ones that are useful to your narrowed topic. If you are going to write mostly about the narrator and Calum, I would suggest that the drowning of their parents was probably the most important single thing in either of their lives.
- Obviously important also, are the visits the narrator makes to his brother, his joining Calum and the others at the mine and his driving Calum back to Cape Breton to die. These events highlight the roles family members play in others' lives.

You can now think about the events and the relationships you have listed in the context of the question and start to shape your argument and your essay.

- Analyse these key events and relationships. What do they have to say about the narrator's understanding of the past and the ways of his family? If you look closely at the relationship between him and Calum *while* considering the key events in their lives, you are likely to conclude that the death of their parents made the lives of the two brothers go in completely separate directions. While his grandparents took in the narrator, Calum had to be the leader of a new, isolated family composed of the three brothers. The way Calum's life turns out is a direct result of his loss.

- Develop an argument to give your response cohesion and structure. Here you could argue that *No Great Mischief* clearly shows that family is critical to survival, the development of life-long relationships and responsibilities, and that its importance is deeply rooted in the patterns of the Scottish heritage of the clan Donald.
- Alternatively, you could argue the opposite!

REFERENCES & FURTHER READING

The Text

MacLeod, Alistair, No Great Mischief, Random House, Sydney, 2001.

Further Reading

Alistair MacLeod has published two books of short stories,

The Lost Salt Gift of Blood and *As Birds Bring Forth The Sun*. Like *No Great Mischief*, these stories are set in Cape Breton. They can be found, along with one previously uncollected story, in the following collection:

MacLeod, Alistair, *Island*, W.W. Norton, New York, 2000.

Websites

http://home.eol.ca/~jarovi/mac_intro.htm (containing an interview by Robert Jarovi with Alistair MacLeod)

http://omega.cc.umb.edu/~irish/macleod.htm

http://www.wwnorton.com/catalog/spring00/04970.htm

http://www.impacdublinaward.ie/2001/nogreatmischief.htm

http://www.randomhouse.com/vintage/read/nogreatmischief/